The Children We Teach

CONDITION: F— (231798)

Edition: 1st   Prtg: 2P   DJ/NO

COMMENTS: (34)

KEYWORDS: DRS 1700, Education, Youth Development, Child Psychology

225 0 2 16

By the same author

An Introduction to Psychology
The Nursery Years
Intellectual Growth in Young Children

The Children We Teach
Seven to Eleven Years

Susan Isaacs

Introduction by Millie Almy

SCHOCKEN BOOKS · NEW YORK

First published 1932
First SCHOCKEN edition 1971

Copyright © 1971 by Schocken Books Inc.
Library of Congress Catalog Card No. 75–139841

*Published by arrangement with the
University of London Press Ltd.*

Manufactured in the United States of America

Second Printing, 1972

TO MELANIE KLEIN
AND M. N. SEARL
WHO UNDERSTAND
THE MINDS OF CHILDREN

Contents

Contents

Chapter 4 · Intellectual Development

Introduction

By the time this edition of *The Children We Teach* is published, over forty years will have elapsed since Susan Isaacs began its formulation. Those years have encompassed World War II, Sputnik, a tremendous upsurge in educational and psychological research, and, especially in the United States, increasingly widespread dissatisfaction with public schooling. The technology of education now includes films, tapes, typewriters, and computers as well as books and magazines. New curricula, some encompassing kindergarten through high school, have been developed by representatives of the various disciplines including mathematics and the physical, biological, and behavioral sciences. Team teaching, aides, new ways of grouping youngsters have been introduced into traditional school organization. Despite all this, for too many children, school has come to represent "death at an early age." Classes for them are humdrum, their teachers dull, learning routine, and intellectual excitement rare or nonexistent.

Some educators, concerned with the all too evident lack of vitality in too many classrooms, have recently discovered the evolution that has been going on in the primary schools in England. Beginning in the infant school (for children ages 4+ to 7+ years) and now extending into the junior school (7+ to 11+ years), as many as 60 per cent, according to one authority, of England's primary schools are moving toward child-centered, activity-based programs that differ rather mark-edly from the textbook-dominated programs that have become typically American.

Susan Isaacs, although she unfortunately did not live long enough to see the expansion of her ideas into widely accepted practice, was a major contributor through her writing, lecturing, and especially through her students, to the transformation of the traditional British primary school. The nature of that contribution, and its relevance to many current problems, will be readily apparent to the present-day reader of *The Children We Teach*. This work, written as a sequel to *The Nursery Years: The Mind of the Child from Birth to Six Years* (Schocken, 1968), follows upon the same theme—that, in fostering the child's emotional and social development, we must not neglect his very real intelligence and powers of observation, his ability to impose his own intellectual order on what he is experiencing. In working with primary-school children, the teacher's aim is once again the development of "the whole child."

While some of the research of the last forty years may well have led Dr. Isaacs to modify certain of her views, she would never minimize the importance of the teacher's knowledge of either the typical trends in intellectual and social development, and their interrelatedness, or the tremendous range of individual differences among children. Nor would she underestimate the complexities of the teacher's role in planning for, as well as with, children to further their development and learning.

In the light of current concern for the adequacy of the intelligence test as a measure of the child's capacity for adaptation, Dr. Isaacs' emphasis on the practical value of the "mental ratio" may seem overstated. Recent research also calls into question her assumption that ability grouping, or, as the British say, "streaming," necessarily facilitates teaching and learning. On the other hand, the kind of collaboration between psychologist and teacher she envisioned for both the interpretation of tests and application of the findings in the classroom is seldom realized in present-day schools.

Dr. Isaacs saw the tests as one means of attuning the teacher to the nature of the child's thinking. She recognized the importance of Piaget's work to such understanding, but she also pointed out the limitations inherent in applying his stage theory (then based largely on studies of the child's verbalization) too literally. In many ways her discussion of the ways the thought of the seven–to–eleven-year-old differs from that of his infant-school contemporary parallels Piaget's more recent distinctions between intuitive and operational thought. But the nature of the problems the child may confront in school is not necessarily dictated by the level of thinking he reveals in test or interview. Rather, in terms prophetic of Jerome Bruner's dictum in *The Process of Education* (1960), Dr. Isaacs notes, "If we make each kind of problem simple enough and clear enough, even children in the Infant School years, will be able to deal with it."

One wonders whether Dr. Isaacs would have been as concerned with what has come to be known as "the problem of the match" as are current educational researchers. Certainly she would have wanted to provide each child with intellectual experience both appropriate to his level of thinking and challenging it. In all probability however, she would have seen this mainly as a matter of, on the one hand, providing opportunity for both activity and discussion and, on the other, knowing the child, his interests and his concerns, as well as his cognitive abilities. For, "It is the child's doing, the child's active social experience and his own thinking and talking that are the chief means of his education."

This is the philosophy that underlies the evolving British primary school. Not without irony, it may be noted that progressive education as it emerged in the United States in the 1930's also embodied this idea—that the active involvement of the child was essential for his proper education. Although there was a later widespread reaction against progressive education, an understanding of child development continued to be regarded as essential to both teaching and curriculum development. Too often, however, it appears that the child was regarded somewhat as a passive receptacle for knowledge whose I.Q. and interests must be taken into account if he were to retain the knowledge provided. The extent to which the child was capable of transforming to his own views, as well as rejecting, whatever the classroom offered received less attention.

We may speculate that, in the United States, the intelligence-testing movement, in which Dr. Isaacs saw such promise, went amiss. Tests multiplied—not only those that were designed to measure intelligence, and individually administered, but tests of readiness, achievement, aptitude, and personality that could be given on a group basis. Thus teachers could share in a tremendous amount of information about the children they taught. But how often they did share, and how often the limitations of the tests were made apparent to them, are open questions. Rarely, one suspects, has a comprehensive testing program been tied to the kind of child study that Dr. Isaacs espoused. As D. E. M. Gardner notes, "She would not have us rely for our knowledge of children entirely on tests and structured situations any more than she would advocate these as being the best situations to encourage young children to function at their highest level."

Proponents of the modern British primary school are convinced that when the primary focus is on the children and their ways of thinking and learning, the school becomes the place where children do function at the highest level. But such function is not, as many of the detractors of progressive education held, a mere matter of letting the child "learn what interests him." Nor is the teacher's role that of passive onlooker. Knowledgeable, not only about children, but also, in varying degrees, about mathematics, science, social and environmental studies, language and the expressive arts, the teacher sets the stage for the children to develop increasing competence in these areas. His involvement with them is active in suggesting, listening, commenting, questioning, speculating, recapitulating, evaluating, instructing, sometimes with an individual, sometimes with a small group, sometimes with the whole class.

The Children We Teach assumes just such a complex and responsible role for the teacher. It is a demanding, challenging role, possible, as Dr. Isaacs suggests, only when the groups of children involved are not too large, or too diverse, and, we would presume, when administrative support is provided for it.

Our schools have suffered under many panaceas in the last forty years. To take the British primary school too literally as a model for American elementary education may be to court further disaster. But to seek and find ways to bring the depth of understanding of children and

their teachers that Susan Isaacs had into present-day
classrooms can surely bring them nothing less than new
vitality and promise.

MILLIE ALMY

Teachers College
Columbia University
July, 1970

Preface

The substance of this book first appeared as a series of twenty-four articles in *The Teacher's World*.

It deals with children of the Primary School ages, i.e., between seven and eleven years. Its aim is to show children, neither as merely illustrating a series of abstract psychological laws, nor as mere creatures-to-be-taught, but as living individuals. I hope that teachers already in the schools, as well as students in training, will find it useful.

SUSAN ISAACS

The Children We Teach

Chapter 1 · Introductory

1. The Teacher, the Child, and the Psychologist

In this book, I am going to write not so much about schools and teaching as about the children who are in the schools. The children themselves are the living aim and end of our teaching. It is their thought, their knowledge, their character and development which make the purpose of our existence as schools and teachers. And it is the modes of their learning and understanding, their physical growth and social needs, which in the end determine the success or failure of our methods of teaching.

It can be fully admitted that the most far-reaching book knowledge of psychology will not of itself ensure practical success in the classroom. No theory of how things should be done can take the place of the intuitive perception and direct response to children which come from native gifts and long experience. Nevertheless, even a first-rate practical teacher can gain something from a study of children's minds for their own sake, and from looking at the general facts of children's thinking and feeling and doing, as these have been gathered together by the psychologist. Let me suggest how some of these gains come about.

The psychologist looks at the development of

children all round and as a whole, not just at the children in this class or that school, or in such and such a town. He notes their modes of learning, their plays and games, the rate of their mental growth, their emotions and thoughts at different ages, in every sort of place and time, and under every sort of education. This wider view of children enables him to see rather more of the broad laws of their development, and to get more sense of the general modes of their growth than can come to the teacher who is kept at close grips with the children of a particular school and neighbourhood. And the psychologist has more leisure to find out what children really are like in themselves, since he is not faced with the practical urgencies of the teacher who has to train them. He can watch and listen to children out of school as well as in it—in the home, the street, the cinema, the public parks, wherever children are to be found. He has ways of comparing and measuring the behaviour of children at different ages and under different conditions which help to make his notes more exact and reliable than ordinary observations can ever be.

On the other hand, although he interests himself in the *general* characteristics of children at different ages, yet when he comes to study individual children as individuals, he can do so more freely and fully than the practical necessities of the educator allow. The class teacher, however adaptable, cannot put the aim of understanding any one child before his practical responsibilities to the group as a whole. But the psychologist is often called upon to make a full and detailed study, with all his scientific resources, of the mind of one child. And so he is sometimes able to discover things which even a skilled and sympathetic class teacher has been at a loss to understand.

One not uncommon example of this can be found in those cases of children who have remained markedly backward in some particular direction, such as reading, in spite of excellent class teaching. A case of this kind came to my notice just recently—a girl of thirteen years, who could read no better than a child of five. This backwardness in reading had naturally acted very adversely on all her school work, and on her general emotional development. She had become difficult and unsatisfactory all round, and was referred for a psychological examination. With a detailed study it became clear that her intelligence was fairly normal, and that the general backwardness was almost entirely due to the influence of the specific failure to progress in the early stages of learning to read. And this in turn showed itself to be quite remediable with special coaching based on a study of the special details of the early difficulty. In a few weeks her reading ability had been brought to the level of a ten-year-old, and there was every prospect of all-round improvement in character and school record.

Another instance of the way in which the technical knowledge of the psychologist can be of aid is the case of a boy of seven who was brought to my own notice by his teacher recently. He was uninterested, backward in every direction, and "wouldn't work". His teacher had not been able to determine whether he was really dull or "just lazy", and was therefore not quite sure how to treat him among the others. After a detailed study with tests of intelligence, it became clear that he was just about average in mental ability, and that there was no reason why the ordinary spurs to effort and attention should not be applied to him. There is, of course, a good deal to be said about "laziness", but at any rate his teacher was now able to feel that she was not wasting her time and demanding things quite out of the child's reach when she tried to keep him up to the standard of work of the class as a whole.

After many such individual studies, the psychologist can sometimes offer practical suggestions which may help to make general teaching methods more elastic and more exact.

In both the above cases we touch upon one of the most important aids which psychology has been able to bring to the practical teacher in recent years—in helping to make clear some of the many different reasons why children may be backward in school work. Later on I shall go more fully into this, and discuss the various causes of backwardness and possible ways of dealing with it.

Another interesting individual problem came my way the other day. I had occasion to ask a girl of six years and a half the meaning of certain words. One of these words was "health", and I was a little startled when she said brightly and confidently, "Health is what you have your teeth out with!" This answer seems to suggest how closely the effects of a teacher's words, and of explanations by grown-ups in general, are limited by the child's own mind. The girl had listened to a number of simple talks about health and how to keep well, and among other things, the importance of caring for the teeth. I am sure that these talks were quite clear and simple enough from all ordinary points of view. But for some individual reason they evidently left only a queer mix-up of ideas in this child's mind. It would have been extraordinarily interesting to find out (as I had no chance to do) just what had caused this muddle—and very illuminating for the teacher who had given the lessons on health.

But it is not only the question of individual needs which is made clearer by knowing something of children's minds as the psychologist sees them. There are many ways in which our notions of what we ought to demand of children generally in the schools (and for that matter in the home) have been altered progressively as our knowledge of children's minds has been added to. Some of these are now of course old history—as, for example, the way in which we discarded long backless benches in schools in favour of the more comfortable dual or single desks, when we came to see that the earlier forms were not only bad for the children's physical growth, but incited fidgets and mischief, and failed to make use of the growing boy's natural sense of pride and ownership in his own possessions. In the same way, we gave up asking little girls in the lower standards to do useless samples of extremely fine needlework, when we came to understand that this was not only very bad for eyes, nerves, and temper, but devoid of interest or meaning or practical value to the child. The capable teacher could always succeed in getting children to do these things, and sometimes to do them astonishingly well; but we have now given up thinking that they are the right things for children to do. Our standards of work for the children, and our practical ideals in the school, have been changed in many directions by our sounder knowledge of what does really help them to grow in skill and knowledge and understanding and health.

One change which is going on at this moment is a further example, viz. language teaching in the lower forms. We are beginning to realise that it is quite useless to expect clear and fluent expression in *writing*, no matter how good our lessons in composition may be, if at the same time we shut out all chance of the child's learning to express himself in *speech*. The silent class-room is the worst possible training for written ex-pression. But children who are encouraged to talk freely in class about things that interest them, to tell stories, to describe and discuss, soon come to *write* with greater ease and aptness and style, as well as to *think* more clearly and accurately. And enterprising schools are beginning to accept this fundamental truth, and to find ways of encouraging speech and using it con-structively.

These are but brief examples of the stimulus and help which the study of the ways of children's growth can bring to the school. I shall offer more such instances as I discuss the various aspects of the mental life of children of Primary School ages. My aim is to help the teacher to renew his insight into the needs of the children he deals with. By lifting his eyes from the immediate practical concerns of the classroom, and borrowing the vision of the psychologist from time to time, the teacher can often gain fresh interest in his pupils as human beings, and increase his own practical resources and adaptability.

2. "And One Man in his Time plays many Parts"

The period of childhood and school life which this book chiefly considers is the middle period, the years from seven to eleven.

> "And then the whining school-boy, with his satchel
> And shining morning face. . . ."

I am going to deal with these years because they are the period of the new Primary Schools. But of course the seven-year-old was six only a little while ago, and the eleven-year-old will soon be twelve. He is the same boy throughout his school life, from the nursery class to the Central or Secondary School— although it may suit us to concentrate our attention upon one period at a time.

Is the division of his life into Nursery, Infants', Primary, and Senior School periods simply one of practical convenience, or has it some inner meaning from the point of view of his own mental growth?

Certainly its main significance is the practical one. There is no sharp line dividing the mind of the six-year-old from that of the seven, nor that of the eleven-year-old boy from his brother of twelve. We know this quite well. Just as we know that the minds of children within these groups do not move forward by sharp stages corresponding to their promotion from one class to another. Standard III children are growing and developing throughout the year, and we hardly imagine that when we promote them to Standard IV their minds make a sudden jump forward too. We find it convenient to mark them off and move them up in these sharp steps, but we know that their mental development itself goes on more or less steadily all the time.

The same is true when the child ceases to be labelled an "infant", and becomes a member of the Primary department; and when he passes from the Primary to the Senior School.

It is as well to remind ourselves of this, because sometimes people tend to have a vague notion that the "Primary" period is very clearly marked in mental growth, as well as in school work. Indeed, our practice has often assumed that there is a sharp mental change in the child at the age when he enters the classes above the Infants'. The sudden contrast between the easy, genial atmosphere and active world of the Infants' School, and the sterner, drier, more formal ways of the Girls' and Boys' departments must often have been very puzzling, and rather trying, to children in the past. It has usually been the most marked external change which the child has undergone through all his school days. Less now than it was, it is still, in many schools, more than it need be or should be.

Yet it is not without a slight degree of justification in the child's own mind. Up to a point, children of, say, six and seven years of age do begin to feel themselves to be leaving the ways of infancy behind, and do seem to want to be treated as more responsible, capable of harder tasks and of higher standards of behaviour. Anyone who has had the opportunity, which I myself have enjoyed, of educating little children under very "free" conditions, knows that at anything over five and a half years, both boys and girls will begin to hanker for what they call a "proper school", where they are "made to work", have definite tasks and much expected of them in the way of self-control. The child of this age in the Kindergarten or Infants' School begins to feel envious of his somewhat older brother, who is treated as more responsible and more grown-up.

A certain hardening in our demands, a certain stiffening in organisation and in the standard of work, at the change-over from the Infants' to the Primary School, undoubtedly finds response in children's own feelings. They like it to be a real change, a real advance.

But it should not be a completely different world that the doors of the Primary department open to Infants' School children. The work and the ways of the new life should link on to the old. The teacher of the lower groups in the Primary School should gather up and use for the children's new needs all that the well-run Infants' School offers her. The gifts of speech and song and dance can still be fruitful. The pleasure of making things, of free expression in dramatic movement, in chalk and paint can be adapted to the new level of learning. The easy, friendly relation between children and teacher need not be lost, even though more be expected from the children.

There is, no doubt, plenty of difference between the children in the middle of the Primary School, at say nine or ten years of age, and the typical child of the Infants' School. Just as there is between the typical Primary School child and the youth or girl of thirteen or fourteen. There *are* characteristic phases of development as children pass from infancy to maturity. And these phases do call for difference in treatment and methods of teaching. But they are not marked off from each other at their boundaries. There is nothing in human development corresponding to the metamorphoses in the life of the insect—the change from the larva to the pupa, from the chrysalis to the butterfly. It is *only* when we take the middle years of each "period" that we can see the characteristic differences in need and in development.

If we keep in mind the fact that in human children the passage from one phase to another is always gradual, we can then usefully go on to consider what the different phases are—the many parts that one man plays.

The most sharply marked crisis in the whole of the child's development after birth is the change-over from true infancy to "toddlerhood". Getting teeth and learning to walk and talk make more difference to the child than anything that happens later on. This change perhaps deserves to be called a crisis, since by it the child ceases to be a wholly dependent and limpet-like creature. He begins to get about the world, which suddenly enlarges its boundaries for him; and he begins to exchange ideas as well as to cry.

For some years, however, he remains intensely dependent in his emotional life upon his father and mother and home circle. From two to five, the years of the new Nursery Schools, he is learning all sorts of bodily skills, gaining much knowledge of the world, and mastering many words and speech forms. He is also going through the most difficult period of his life in emotional development and social learning. At about five to six years he begins to settle down into childhood proper, when his interests turn more freely to things and people outside his home, and he becomes less acutely dependent upon sheltering adults.

There would thus not seem to be any well-marked psychological phases corresponding *exactly* to the division of school life into the Nursery School, the Infants' School, and the Primary School. This educational grouping is largely due to the accidents of history. Children differ quite a good deal as to the exact age when they win the relative independence of childhood—it may be at anything from five to seven years. It is very probable that the soundest educational plan would be to carry the typical ways of the Nursery School on through the Infants' School period too, making a gradual year-by-year change, however, in the direction of Primary School methods.

After the passage from toddlerhood to childhood proper, no other well-marked phase of change can be made out (although change is always going on, now in this direction, now in that), until the beginning of puberty. The margins of this phase again vary from child to child, but may be set at roughly twelve to thirteen years. Puberty in boy or girl marks the beginning of sexual maturity; but only the beginning. It is still many years before full maturity of mind and body is reached—during the period we call adolescence.

The years of the Primary School thus do not correspond exactly, limit by limit, to such true phases of change in mind and body as can be discovered. These years fall at both ends within the true psychological period of childhood which lies between toddlerhood and puberty. This gives us another reason for emphasising the importance of linking up very closely the methods and curriculum of the Primary School with what comes before and what is to follow.

And of these two links the earlier is the more important. The child of eleven can deal better than the seven-year-old with a sharp contrast in his educational environment. Such a marked change (if itself in the right direction) may indeed prove for him a stimulus and a tonic. But the child in the lower groups of the Primary School is barely different from what he was in the upper classes of the Infants' School. His needs of body and mind have hardly changed at all. And to make the most of his first year or two in the new life calls for free co-operation between the two departments, and a full understanding of each other's aims and methods.

Chapter 2 · Individual Differences

1. One Child and Another

I have glanced briefly at the fact that there are certain broad characteristic differences between children of different ages. In the later pages of this book I shall attempt to fill in some of the details of the picture of the Primary School period of development.

But before I do this there is another set of facts to consider, viz. the facts of *individual differences*. We all know that children of any given period differ much amongst themselves. The "Primary School child" as such is only a lay figure, convenient for us to hang our educational generalisations upon. But Tommy Smith and Mary James and Dick Harrison, all ten years of age last month, have almost as many differences as likenesses. Tommy is pinched and undersized and backward; Mary is quick and talkative, but not very reliable; Dick is steady and capable and shaping for a scholarship. And these contrasts in ability and temperament make them far from easy to deal with in one class and by the same methods. It is little use expecting Tommy to keep up with the general level of his group, whereas Dick forges ahead of it without trouble, and Mary gets restless and mischievous, because she has not enough to keep her busy while the needs of the bulk of the class are being met.

The actual differences between Tommy and Mary and Dick, as the teacher finds them, are the end result of three main sorts of influence. First, and probably foremost in importance, there is the original difference in inborn ability between child and child. This sets the limit of possibility beyond which we cannot teach the child. We are very familiar with this limit in the case of those children who have been picked out for Special Schools. We know that even the most skilful ways of teaching will never bring them up to the educational level of the average ordinary child. And the ordinary child has his limits too, fortunately very much higher and wider in range; but none the less fixed by his original mental equipment.

Even if a child has a very high intellectual ability, however, he may never be able to reap the fruit of his original gifts, unless he also has certain qualities of temperament and character. If he cannot persevere in his work, if he is unstable in his aims and wishes, if he settles into perverse ways in school, his mother wit will not carry him very far in actual learning and doing. The child who is a little less intelligent, but steadier and more willing to work, may sometimes go farther in school and in later life than the clever but unstable. Those who go farthest of all have high intelligence *plus* grit and steadiness and persistent aims.

Amongst any group of children of these years, there will be found all sorts of temperaments and social qualities—cheerful and friendly, lively and pert, lethargic and heavy, sly or contrary, enterprising, docile, and placid. Whatever the medley of personalities may be, the successful teacher learns to know them all, and to handle each child so as to keep the general life of the class going smoothly. Yet each child's particular needs have to be met, too, if the general level is to be kept as high as it might be.

The third sort of influence which makes for differences among the children is found in their homes and general social background. One child will come from a home where there are books and talk, excursions and holidays, and where father and mother take an intelligent interest in the child's friendships and school progress. Another will come from an almost illiterate family life; a third from an overcrowded tenement where nearly every need of childhood is neglected. And between these there will be all varieties of goodness and badness, of help and hindrance. All these things considered together, it is little wonder that the children of a Primary School vary so widely in educational record.

One child turns to books naturally, as a source of pleasure and information. To another, it never occurs that such things as books exist anywhere but in school; to a third, they are things of no value; and a fourth will never be able to learn their intelligent use. The first child has a wide and flexible vocabulary, and easy ways of expression in speech or writing, even before we have begun to teach him anything; a second may be quick at picking up our ways of speech—but as a foreign language, belonging to the world of school, and having nothing to do with the world of home or street; a third remains meagre in words and dull in their use—whether by natural defect or poor home surroundings, it may be hard for the teacher to guess.

The children who are used to books and to discussions at home will bring a much wider background of general knowledge to their school work in, for example, English and history and geography. And if they are themselves able and intelligent, they will move easily forward in all these fields. Their spontaneous interests will be much wider and more varied than those of the child of poorer intelligence or a meaner home. The knowledge they gain in schools will be less likely to remain stuck in watertight compartments. They will more readily see the links between one group of facts and another—between history and geography, between handwork and arithmetic and geometry. And in this way, each single subject will make a bigger contribution to their general understanding than with the child of poorer native ability, who learns each fact as an isolated thing, unless links are laboriously forged for him; or than the child from an ignorant home, who brings no nurtured interests with him to school.

The more intelligent child, or the one in whose home the intelligent use of books and newspapers and talk is an everyday affair, will be able to do much more for himself in school. He will not need to be so carefully spoon-fed, nor so often prodded, in order to get on.

In a host of ways these contrasts of social setting, of temperament, and of inborn ability, will show themselves amongst the children we teach. They set the class teacher a very hard task, unless the school finds some method of assorting the children so as to lessen the differences found in any one group.

It is with this in mind that many head teachers are

now beginning to use the native intellectual ability of the children as expressed in "mental age" as the chief basis of grading classes. Of all the differences between one child and another, inborn intelligence turns out to be the most stable and permanent. It is the most significant for success in school and career. The best teaching in the world may prove barren if it fall on the stony ground of an inherently dull and lifeless mind. And we cannot cater properly for the brightest and the stupidest children together in one class.

Inborn ability could not be used as the *sole* basis of grading, of course, for differences in actual years, in home circumstances, and in temperament do also count heavily. But all those people who have been using mental age, rather than birthday age, as the *main* basis of grading, have found that the work both of individual children and of the school as a whole has greatly benefited. Such a classification makes it so much more possible to give to each according to his needs.

2. How we measure the Differences between Children

Now this problem of individual differences in native ability is far more bothersome in the Primary School, especially in its earlier years, than in the Infants' School or the Senior department. It is not so troublesome in the Infants' classes, because children under seven do not yet show such wide differences. If we measure what all the six-year-olds and all the ten-year-olds can do, we shall find a bigger *range* of differences among the older group. The duller ones will be farther behind the general level, the brighter children farther ahead of it, than in the earlier age.

On the other hand, if we turn to children in the Senior, Central, or Secondary Schools, we shall find those in any one group sticking closer to the average level of the group than in the Primary School classes. But this is for quite a different reason from that which explains the same fact in the Infants' School. If we were to take a very large group of the older children, from all sorts of schools and places, and study what they could do, we should find even greater differences among them than with the ten-year-olds. The actual range of variation, both in intelligence and in scholastic record, goes on increasing with the years of development. But by one means or another, the eleven-year-olds and over get sorted out into separate groups roughly corresponding to their ability. The more intelligent are picked out by scholarship promotion or selection for a Secondary School. It is true that there are intelligent children left even then in the elementary standards, as everyone knows; but the proportion is smaller, and the best not quite so good.

And at the other end of the scale, the mentally defective children have dropped out of the general stream. It is in the Primary School, before all these selective agencies have been at work, that the teacher has to cope with the largest range and variety of differences in any one class. It is here that it is most necessary for the Head to find such ways of grading the children as will lessen these great practical difficulties for the class teacher.

How then can we measure the differences between

one child and another, in respect of their innate ability, leaving out all the accidental differences due to home circumstances, to knowledge gained in school, and to good or bad methods of teaching?

One of the first people to ask this very practical question was a French psychologist, Alfred Binet. Binet published his first scale of "mental tests" in 1908. Since that day many psychologists all over the world have given time and attention to this problem, but Binet's tests remain the most widely used and the most generally useful way of comparing one child with another in respect of intelligence, particularly in the Primary School years. Not, however, in their first form. Binet himself and his collaborator Simon revised the tests as first published; and an American investigator, Terman, has suggested many additions and improvements which have been widely accepted by those using the tests. Professor Burt has further adapted the details and the wordings of the tests for use with English children.

The general aim of these tests is to measure intelligence "as such"; that is to say, to find out what the child can do with the information he may have, rather than to gauge the information itself. But of course we cannot measure intelligence in a vacuum. All we can do is to put problems to the child at any given age which assume for their solution only such a minimal amount of knowledge as he must by that age (in all ordinary circumstances) have managed to get, unless he be very backward. If, for instance, a child of nine years who has had ordinary schooling cannot make up a sentence containing three simple words given to him; if at eight years he cannot tell us any of the similarities between an apple and an orange, nor give an intelligible account of what he would do if he broke something belonging to another person; if at ten years he cannot explain *why* it is absurd for the soldier to say "I am writing this letter with a sword in one hand and a pistol in the other"—then he must lack to a greater or less degree that ability to profit by experience which is one of the things we mean by intelligence. (We should not judge him on any one of these problems, needless to say; they are but illustrations of the sort of thing which the child is asked to do.)

Should he be a gipsy child, or have his home on a canal-boat, and thus have largely escaped schooling, then these particular tests would not be very valuable. We have to find other tests for such children. But when applied to ordinary children going to school at the ordinary ages, such questions do serve to bring out differences in the ability to make use of experience.

From the few examples quoted it will be seen that there is nothing elaborate or secret or strange about the actual tests themselves. The questions are mostly of a kind very similar to those which children have to deal with in the ordinary business of their lives. The difference between a scientific scale of mental tests and any ingenious questions which anyone might choose to put to a child lies entirely in the fact that the scale has itself been *standardised*. That is to say, it has been tried out on a very large number of children of all ages, under similar conditions. The average performance of the children of each age with each item of the scale has thus been discovered. Moreover, the extent to which success or failure in each single test tends to go along with success or failure in the other tests has been noted. And the degree to which the results of the tests hang together with the teachers' judgment of the children's ability, based on classroom observation and scholastic record, has been ascertained.

By using all these different sources of information, comparing them with the aid of exact statistical methods, we have been able to reject or alter the details of the tests as was needed. And we have thus arrived at a fairly reliable scale of tests representing the *norm* of mental development for each chronological age. When, therefore, the psychologist says that a child of a certain age should be able to pass such and such a test, what he means is not that this is morally or educationally desirable, but that a high percentage (roughly 70 per cent.) of the children who reached that age last birthday do in fact pass the test. (That is to say, in any *large random* group of children.)

The brighter children of any particular birthday age, however, are able to deal with tests suitable for the average child of older years. This is what we mean by "mental age". A child of eight who succeeds on all the tests meant for ten-year-olds has a "mental age" of ten. If he fails on the tests for his own age, and succeeds only with the six-year tests, then his mental age is six. Mental age has turned out to be a most convenient way of expressing the difference between one child's intellectual ability and another's.

Even more useful and significant is the measure we call the "mental ratio" or "intelligence quotient". This is the ratio between mental age and birthday age, taking the mental age as numerator and chronological age as denominator. For the practical purposes of education, there is a vast difference between two children of the mental age of eight, one of whom is ten, and the other only six years of chronological age. The first child comes quite close to the border of actual mental defect. The second has an intelligence of a high order, and is likely to go far in the world of knowledge.

But it is time I clothed these dry bones of theoretical discussion with the behaviour of living children. If we look in some detail at the different ways in which children of different mental ratio respond to our teaching, we shall get a more vivid sense of the great significance of what we mean by mental ratio. Before going on to do this, however, I must speak a word of caution.

The actual giving of the tests is, in spite of their apparently simple nature, a highly expert and technical job. If we want trustworthy information about a child's success in the tests, then the manner of giving them, and all the general conditions, must be exactly the same for all children tested. We have to be able to get the best performance of which the child is capable by his own efforts, without giving him any hint or help. And to do this is a fine art. It takes much time and training and experience to learn where the possible snags are and how to avoid them. If given by an untrained amateur, the test results will be inaccurate and worthless.

Those who are actively interested in the possibility of making use of mental tests as an aid to classification should not rush in to apply them immediately without training. (It would indeed be a pity even to try out for fun or curiosity the examples I have quoted above, for that would only spoil them for use with those children by a trained person.)

The wisest thing would be to take advantage of one of the courses in mental testing arranged by the National Institute of Industrial Psychology, or by some of the more enterprising Local Education Authorities. With the help of such training, the practical value to the teacher of the standardised tests of intelligence would soon be made clear.

3. Some Children

Having got some notion of the general meaning of "mental ratio" and how it is measured, let us look at a few individual children of different mental levels, and see what the differences in behaviour are.

Here is John, aged seven years and ten months, not yet moved up from the Infants' department because he is a year and a half behind in his school work. He is described as "very dull", and he looks it, drooping his head, peering dully out under his brows, moving lifelessly. A small smile can be brought to his face by an encouraging remark, but he shows no fun, no enterprise, no active interest in the world. Sitting at the table with me, he counts thirteen pennies correctly, names four of the commonest coins, shows that he knows right from left, says what is missing in a series of faces drawn with either an eye, nose, or mouth left out, answers certain simple practical questions, and says certain words after me. He does, in sum, all the tests appropriate to the age of six. But on the other hand he fails on two of the five-year tests. He cannot remember and carry out three simple commissions on hearing the instructions once, nor give definitions of common objects in the way usually done by children of five years. However, he succeeds with two of the seven-year tests. He is able to describe what he sees in certain pictures, and to copy the drawing of a diamond-shaped figure. But on the other problems for this year, and all the later ones, he fails. He cannot, for example, say how many fingers he has on both hands, nor tie a bow-knot, nor give the differences between certain everyday things. His mental age comes out at exactly six years (the two seven-year successes making up for the two five-year failures), and his mental ratio at 77 (mental age ÷ chronological age × 100). He thus turns out to be very near the administrative borders of mental deficiency, and one is not surprised at the degree of his retardation in school work.

John, as we said, looks dull. But here is Mark, reported by his teacher to be also one year behind in work, who by no means looks dull. He has the bluest of blue eyes, rosy cheeks, and a good-natured cheerful smile for all the world. He gives his name clearly when asked, and says he is six. His age is six years and ten months. He is eager to "play games" with me, and wants "to come first", before the other boys. All he can do in the tests he does with zest and enjoyment, but he is quite oblivious of his failures (these are never pointed out by the tester). He succeeds with only four of the five-year tests, failing to pick out the heavier of two blocks which look alike, and to give definitions of common objects. His way of failing on this last test is itself very interesting. Most children of five, if asked "What's a chair?" will say "To sit on," or "You sit on it." Mark just pointed to a chair with a pleased grin, and said nothing. When asked "What's a horse?" he pointed to a picture of a horse that happened to be on the wall; and so with five of the six objects mentioned. The sixth, a fork, was not to be seen, and so he was quite at a loss—but he smiled cheerfully all the same!

Now at first sight it might seem to be a sign of intelligence to point out the thing itself when asked "What's a chair?" And so it would be in a three-year-old. But if a child of five years and over takes the question "What is a chair?" as being equivalent to "Show me a chair," then he has obviously not reached the intellectual level proper to his age. His thought is still tied to the *here* and *now* of perception. It has not reached the level of an *idea*. The child has not formed a concept of the chair, but merely attached a verbal label to the concrete object. And thus he is quite at a loss when the thing itself is not present, and cannot make any communication about it.

Mark cannot distinguish between right and left, nor count thirteen pennies, nor answer simple practical problems. He passes only two of the six-year tests, and three of the seven-year. He can say how many fingers he has, repeat five numbers after me, and copy the drawing of a diamond. But there he stops, in spite of cheerful trying. His mental age is five and a half years, his ratio 80. He is scarcely less backward than John, in spite of his more attractive appearance and agreeable ways.

These two boys form a striking illustration of how little we can rely upon appearance as an index of mental level. It was at one time believed that mental defect and dullness were always accompanied by physical signs, but we know now that this is by no means true, and that it is safer to measure intelligence directly. The only reliable way of judging a child's ability is to set him problems to do, and watch how he does them relatively to his age.

But let us now see what another seven-year-old does. Fred is nearly the same age as John, seven years and nine months. He is in Standard II, and doing well. He is quiet but responsive and pleasantly mannered. He goes about our problems steadily, and his first failure is on the last of the eight-year tests, a vocabulary test, in which he does not give the meaning of quite the required number of words. He comes down on two of the nine-year problems too, but succeeds with all the ten-year tests except one (again the vocabulary), and does three eleven-year and one twelve-year test. This last is the "interpretation" of the pictures that at an earlier age are merely "described". He does this successfully and interestingly. Together his successes bring his mental age to ten years, and his ratio to 129. Think of teaching a class which includes boys like John and others as able as Fred! How can a teacher meet the needs of both properly? How can she even ensure that both are fully occupied all the time? An oral lesson of value to the Freds will be miles above the heads of the Johns. A demonstration of some simple step in number suitable for the Johns will leave the Freds bored and restless.

This John and this Fred were not in fact in the same school. But I have found even bigger differences in the one class. Among the recent records which I turn up as I write, for example, are those of one class in which the following were the mental ratios of the first half-dozen children I tested in the class: 74, 87, 104, 121, 143, 99. The child of 143, a quiet sweet-faced little girl, has a mind of rare order. Mental ratios of over 140 are few and far between, and of the greatest intellectual promise. There is a career to be watched, and a splendid educational opportunity! What worlds away from the poor feeble intelligences represented by the figures at the lower end of the group!

Here in another school is Mollie, a bright-eyed, freckled girl of nine years and two months. She is picked out by her teacher as among the most intelligent of her class, and a probable scholarship child. She talks easily and happily, follows up ideas started by some of the tests, and tells me about her home and her games and the things she likes best in school. Her face lights up with the delight of understanding when she meets a problem she can do, and she enjoys the effort of even those that are beyond her. She passes easily through all the tests of her age, all but one of the ten and eleven-year group, three of the twelve-year and two of the thirteen, one of the fourteen, two of the sixteen-year or "average adult" tests, and even one of the eighteen or "superior adult" group. When she masters the code which forms one of the sixteen-year tests, she tells me how she and her sister have made up a written "secret language" in their play at home. And when in the vocabulary test she is able to give me the meaning of "lecture", she says "I know that, because my Daddy goes to lectures, and once he took me to one." I get the sense of an intelligent home, where there is talk and wide interests. Her father is a french polisher, and she can tell me something of his work. Her mental ratio is 139.

But free speech in a child does not always mean intelligence, any more than an attractive appearance does. Indeed, it sometimes covers up stupidity, even from the teacher's gaze. Bessie, in the same school, is eight years and three months, and was picked out for me by her teacher as of more than average ability. She talks fluently, and is quite at home with me at once. She even tells me, with an amusingly confidential air, a riddle about "a copper", making play with the two meanings of a penny and a policeman, when she comes to this word in the vocabulary test. Nevertheless, she is thoroughly stupid, her mental ratio being only 77. She makes the wildest shots at answering every question asked, and is quite devoid of self-criticism or any patience or understanding. Her glibness of speech and general air of liveliness had thus quite deceived her teacher (who had not been with the class very long, it is true), but of course they would not carry her far in the more solid work of her later school years.

Last of all, let us look at Maggie, a child of eleven years and three months, large and physically developed, looking almost a grown woman. Her features are well formed, but her expression heavy and unresponsive. She fails on one of the seven-year and two of the eight-year tests, and thereafter succeeds only with two of the nine-year and one of the ten-year tests. Her mental age is just eight, and her mental ratio as low as 71. She is in the same class as our bright nine-year-old Mollie, the children in this school being graded roughly on attainments. But of course she is well behind Mollie and the other bright children in the work of her class, and how different are her responses to what the teacher puts before the group!

4. "Mental Ratio" and its Practical Value

Having looked at the behaviour of certain individual children of different mental ratio, it will now be useful to turn back for a time to general considerations.

I have already pointed out that a child's mental ratio, when properly measured, is one of the most stable and permanent things about him. The re-testing of children at regular intervals over considerable periods of time—six years, with some investigators—has shown that intelligence as expressed in mental ratio remains on the whole remarkably constant throughout the years of development. Changes do occur in some cases, sometimes up, sometimes down, but they are never very marked, and tend to be the exception. The general evidence leads us to believe that a child who starts by being on the dull side of average is most likely to stay there all his life, and the child who begins above the normal is never likely to drop below it. One may show up in different years a little less or a little more intelligent, but will hardly drop or rise right out of one's original group of defective, dull, average, or superior. That is what makes it so useful to discover a child's mental ratio, at any rate by the end of his Infants' School days. The amount of knowledge he may show at any time will depend upon his opportunities in home and school as well as upon his own gifts. His intelligence as measured by standardised tests, however, is very largely independent of chance and opportunity, of good or bad teaching. It seems to be in the main a matter of biological inheritance. If one wants to be a really intelligent person, it is far more important to choose one's parents well than one's schoolmasters!

Mental ratio as measured by a skilled investigator, moreover, turns out to be a more trustworthy index than the teacher's general impression of a child, or even than his actual school record. Taken as a whole, teachers' estimates do tend to be sound and reliable. Taken as a whole, school careers are a safe index of ability. But every now and then the teacher may make a mistake—as, for instance, with the child whose fluent speech and lively manner cover up a great deal of silliness, like the one I quoted above; or with the slow, ponderous but reliable child who will never shine in a group. Sometimes if a child's general personality is not attractive to a particular teacher, or if teacher and child have somehow got across each other, the teacher may tend to underestimate the child's gifts. A gifted but "temperamental" child may do badly with one teacher although well with another. He may be put off his stride through failure to get on with the other children in his class, or through unhappy home circumstances. Illnesses will affect his school record directly and indirectly, far more readily than they will his test performance. Or a child may be doing badly in school because he is wrongly graded. If he is in a class where things are too easy for him, he may fail through boredom and contempt. If they are too hard, he may be thought much more stupid than he really is.

In any or all of such cases, intelligence tests properly given by an experienced person will reveal the genuine ability of the child and show how circumstances had best be altered. There are a large number of cases now on record of such discrepancies between test results and school records, or test results and people's general opinions of a child, where action has been taken on the basis of the tests, with the happiest outcome.

It is thus at the very least worth while testing children at the beginning of their Primary School life, so that any anomalies in the children's attainments due to special circumstances such as those mentioned can be corrected.

But nowadays it is reasonable to say more than this, and to urge that ability as expressed in mental ratio is the soundest general basis for classifying the children in the Primary Schools. Some of the more progressive and informed Local Education Authorities are beginning to encourage this view, and to offer their Heads and assistants the chance of learning the technique of testing intelligence for this purpose.

The children of roughly average ability tend to find their educational level under any system of classification. If in a school one picks out all the children of the middle run of intelligence, those say with mental ratios of 95–110, and inquires what groups they are working in, it is seldom that any are found in a grade much higher or much lower than their age group. And our methods of teaching and general school conditions are well adapted to the needs of the average mass.

It is the dull children and the bright children who are more often to be found in the educational shallows —or out of their depth. And nowadays, far more frequently the bright ones. So much attention has been given to dull and backward children in recent years that we have grown skilled in picking them out, and take it as a matter of course that they need special grouping and special care. The supernormal child, however, has not yet come into his own. There is still a steady drag back on the brighter children towards the level of the mediocre. As Dr. Ballard has put it, "There is little doubt that our school system favours the detecting of the dullard and the overlooking of the genius. It is easy for the brilliant boy to conceal his intelligence; it is difficult for the dunce to conceal his dullness."[1]

Many schools which have come awake to this problem have been trying to cope with it by introducing individual work for their pupils. And individual work (on Dalton lines or other) does help a very great deal. There is much to be said about this, and I mean to discuss the question of individual work very shortly. But no school could be run without some collective teaching and collective occupations. Nor would it be desirable to run it so. Group teaching and common pursuits have a most important place in the education of children in the Primary Schools. They make the right background and general setting for individual work and personal progress. But as soon as children come together in groups, some mode of choosing the groups has to be found.

[1] P. B. Ballard, *Group Tests of Intelligence*, p. 229.

Now it is clear that no single basis of classification can be used alone. Teachers are already used to making exceptions, whether they have been grouping children mainly on their birthday age or mainly on their attainments. Exceptions and qualifications always will have to be made, now in this child's favour, now in that. But all things considered, it seems clear that the most useful primary classification in the Primary School years would be according to mental ratio.

The most practicable details of such a mode of classification have yet to be worked out. They would obviously vary with the size and the general conditions of the school. I cannot do better than offer Dr. Ballard's general suggestions. "There should," he thinks, "be distinct streams of promotion through the school—three is a convenient number—and the factor that should decide in which stream the pupil should be placed can be no other than his mental ratio or intelligence quotient. No other factor tells so much about him; no other factor is so vital and so intimate, so fruitful a source of suggestion, so valid a ground of inference. It should prevail over every other consideration in setting the pupil's general status in the school community. It alone indicates the lines of cleavage between the intellectual levels of the pupils; and without the knowledge it supplies we are limited to a single line of progress through the school. And with a single line of progress through the school it is impossible to solve the problem of the old dull boy and the young bright boy.

"Let it not be thought that in advocating a triple

current of promotion I propose that each class or standard should appear in triplicate. The ordinary standards fit the middle stream; they do not fit either the fast or the slow. Besides, none but the very largest schools could supply enough children to fill the three channels. What I suggest for the school of ordinary size is that each class should have its three sections, the fast, the medium, and the slow; and each section have its own syllabus. The normal line of progress would be from a given section of one class to the corresponding section of the next."[1]

Here, at any rate, is a most fruitful and extraordinarily interesting field for experiment. Among the many possibilities which are giving new life and a new zest to the schools of to-day, none is of greater interest or greater promise than this one.

In this very brief discussion of the nature and practical values of mental tests, I have not tried to do more than provoke the interest of my readers, and to suggest how very useful such tests are as auxiliaries in the school. It would, of course, be quite impossible in so limited a space to go into the technique of giving the tests. I have tried to indicate the very great importance of this technique, and the essential need for training in it. Mental tests are far from "fool-proof", and must never be thought of as a simple foot-rule to be applied mechanically by anyone. They are of value only in the hands of a trained and experienced person, alive to all the possibilities of error, and knowing how to avoid them. Opportunities for getting such training and experience are, however, likely to increase in the

---

[1] P. B. Ballard, *Group Tests of Intelligence*, pp. 232–3.

not distant future. And meanwhile, it is something to
see this new horizon opening before us.

5. Individual Work

I referred above to the recent developments in individual work in the schools. I want now to speak of
some of the psychological facts which justify this
development. I am not going to deal with any details
of method, for the people actually using these methods
in the school can do that far better than I. But it may
be helpful to any teachers who are experimenting with
individual methods of work, or wondering whether
to experiment with them, if we look briefly at a few of
the considerations of fact which underlie them. It is
important to know that the fashion for individual work
has a sound psychological root, and is not a mere
whim of to-day, to be discarded to-morrow.

As we have seen, the major difference between one
child and another lies in his level of general ability. But
even when we are testing him for mental ratio by the
Binet scale, we turn up many other differences which
cannot be expressed in bare mental ratio. Some of these
may be full of meaning for his practical school work,
and illuminating for his teacher.

Take, in the first instance, these two children, of
much the same age and approximately equal mental
ratio. Martha is eight years and eight months old, and
her mental ratio is 116. Peggy is eight years and four
months old, and her mental ratio is 118. This equality
in ratio, however, covers up a very interesting difference. Martha's 116 is gained by succeeding with tests

which lie rather close together on the scale. She does all the nine-year tests, two of the ten-year, and three of the eleven; and this closes her record. But Peggy's 118 is reached by a much more widely scattered series of successes. After passing all the six-year tests, she has some failures and some passes with each following year right up to and including the twelfth. There she succeeds once, but fails on everything beyond. In other words, her successes spread sporadically over six years after the last year which she passes completely. Whereas Martha's spread is but two years.

Clearly if one wants to understand the respective minds of these two children, one needs to know this difference in the scatter of their ability, no less than the equality of their mental ratios when successes and failures are totalled.

Here are further examples: Mary, aged seven years and eleven months, has a mental ratio of 103. After passing all the seven-year tests, she scores sporadically in three further years. Jane's mental ratio is 104; but her successes are scattered over five different years (beginning with the year of her first failure). And Sam gives us a still more interesting example. His mental and chronological ages are just the same, eight years and two months, his ratio thus being dead on the 100. But his successes and failures are spread out over seven successive years (always beyond the last year completely achieved). Such a very wide scatter is, however, unusual. A certain amount of spread—two to four years, say—is quite ordinary. For what we call intelligence expresses itself in many and varied ways, and the Binet scale makes use of a wide variety of mental operations. (This will have been seen from the examples I have quoted here and there.) A scatter of successes over six or seven years is, however, not common.

We are naturally provoked to ask what it may mean. And the answer seems to be that it may mean either or both of two things: (*a*) the partial intervention of a special ability or disability of an intellectual order— for instance, the memory for numbers, visual memory for form, or the gift of words; and (*b*) temperamental instability. Which of the two it means in any particular case can be told partly from the child's behaviour in the test situation, partly from looking at the particular tests on which he succeeds or fails.

To speak first of the temperamental problem. If we find that a child passes a test in a later year of the same sort as he has failed on in an earlier test-year—for instance, the repetition of a series of numbers in reversed order, of a series of syllables, or of the comprehension of simple practical problems—then it is clear that the earlier failure was not due to real intellectual inability, but rather to some inhibition from emotional sources.

Now the whole art of the tester is directed to putting a child at his ease in the test situation, and it is safe to say that if in the hands of an experienced practical psychologist the child's test results are erratic in this way, his behaviour in ordinary life is likely to be even more so. And we do find that the children whose failures are very unevenly spread about the age scale tend to be generally unstable in temperament, especially if these go much below their chronological age. These children are often nervous, sensitive, and easily affected by their emotional environments. If they happen to be highly gifted, they may do brilliantly under favourable conditions, but cannot always be relied upon to live up to their reputations in school work and examinations. They seem to be very often the children who may do well with one teacher, but not so well with another who is less understanding and sympathetic. And it is with children of this type that the highest art of the psychologist is needed to get a true mental ratio, representative of the child's real ability.

It is not only the child with a wide scatter of ability, however, who reveals himself in the way he responds to the test situation. Every child does so, of course. We see the greatest variation in mode of attack and in general behaviour. One child is impetuous and eager, anxious to solve every problem, hungry for praise. Occasionally a child is so impetuous that he may handicap himself by not listening to the instructions or not giving himself long enough to lay hold of a problem before he essays to deal with it. Another will be slow and steady, never wasting a word, and weighing each deliberately before he says it. One child will show himself able to judge his own efforts and appraise his own results; another will be quite devoid of self-criticism or of any objective standard of success. One will be persistent in his attempts to solve a difficult question; another will give up at the least sense of failure. One will be friendly and easy and unafraid of the novel situation; another will tremble with his fear of failure or judgment.

Every teacher knows how these differences in temperament will affect the way children respond to her calls on them and to the group life; and the successful class teacher finds ways of dealing with the different responses. The study of temperament and personality is receiving a good deal of attention from psychologists, and many interesting researches are going on. There is not yet, however, very much scientific knowledge to offer having any detailed practical bearing on the work of the classroom. Tests of temperament are being devised and perfected. And the day may not be far distant when they will be sufficiently reliable for practical use. The wise teacher has at present to rely upon her own direct observations to know how best to handle each child, and much time has to be spent in the winning of such knowledge through the experience of weeks and months. The time may come when tests of temperament, applied to each child individually when he enters the Primary School, either by a psychologist or by a teacher specially trained for the work, might save this waste of time and many mistakes.

For the moment, what can be said is that these differences of temperament are as real and as significant as intellectual differences, and that they must be taken into account by the teacher. They confirm the need for elastic methods in the school, and for individual treatment of children. The appeals which stimulate one child to effort may not be the most fruitful with another. Here a word of praise is needed, there one of criticism; here more positive suggestion, there a greater freedom of initiative. And individual methods of work make this personal adaptation far more easily possible.

To return now to the other possible factor in the scatter of successes and failures on the Binet scale. This takes us into a very large and important field, the study of specific abilities and disabilities. The particular nature of his special gifts and defects may have almost as far-reaching an influence upon a child's scholastic career and after life as his level of general intelligence. If for instance his memory for numbers should be exceptionally poor, his progress in arithmetic may be tardy even though he can reason well—especially if the defect is not discovered and special help given.

There has been great argument amongst psychologists as to whether or not there was such a thing as "general intelligence", or whether after all we were not made up of a large number of specific abilities for this, that, and the other thing, all quite separate and independent of each other. A vast number of experiments have been made to clear this up, and their results have been interpreted now in this way and now in that, as the argument moved back and forth. At this date it is, however, possible to say that the general weight of opinion is in favour of the view that there *is* a something which can be called general intelligence (Professor Spearman preferring to name it by a mere mathematical symbol, *g*, which commits him to no particular theory as to what *g* is); *and* that there are also a great variety of specific abilities (Spearman's *s*). And both *g* and some particular *s* enter into any particular skill we can show or any problem we can solve.

Technical and abstract as this conclusion may seem when stated in this way, it has quite important practical bearings, and many interesting applications to life and education.

The *specific factors* in the child's various performances enter into his success with the individual items of the

Binet scale, but even more powerfully into every aspect
of his school work. His actual level of performance—
whether it be in music or mathematics, carpentry or
modelling, football or dancing, writing essays or
marshalling the facts of geography and history—is the
complex resultant of these two factors, *g* and *s*, his
general intelligence and this, that, or the other specific
ability. In some activities *g* is dominant, in others, *s*.
Of less importance than general ability, specific gifts
may nevertheless have far-reaching effects upon scholastic achievements.

Of the experimental and mathematical devices by
which the distinctive effects of *g* and *s* are studied, I have
no space to speak. One of the most interesting facts
which has come out as the result of recent experiment
is that our specific abilities are far *more* specific than we
used to think. Psychologists used to talk at length, for
example, about *Memory*, whether it was good or bad,
how best to train it, and so on. In school and in ordinary
life we still do so—and even psychologists still find
themselves doing so in their less technical moments.
But in fact we have found that a child (or a grown-up)
cannot really be said to have "a good memory" or "a
bad memory", nor, for that matter, "*a* memory" at all.
He has many sorts of memories, and some may be good
and others bad. He may be very poor at remembering
words or numbers by hearing, for instance, and good at
remembering them by their look as written. He may be
bad at recalling an unconnected series of sounds like a
list of numbers, and good at remembering connected
material such as the gist of a passage he has just read.
He may remember easily and infallibly what he has just

immediately learnt, but not retain and reproduce it well after an interval of time. He may have an excellent memory for the smallest detail of fact in a subject which he has made his own and which holds his interest—and quite useless at remembering things unconnected with this. The head master who can never remember to post his wife's letters may all the same have an unfailing memory for the details of the personal record of every child in his school. The boy who cannot remember dates in history may know exactly where he found the hedge-sparrow's nest in the lane last year when he goes to look for it this spring. Now, as these last examples suggest, such specific kinds of memory are partly a function of interest; but at least certain special memories seem to be a matter of innate gift or defect. And some of these have their effect on the very beginnings of the child's learning in school.

The same sort of thing is true of "the imagination". We sometimes talk about "cultivating the child's imagination" as if this were a single entity or one simple mental process. And yet it is in fact highly complex, with many different aspects. We can distinguish in the first place between the merely reproductive imagination—seeing in the mind's eye pictures or places or people, the inward hearing of voice or orchestra, and so on; and the constructive imagination of the artist, the poet, or the scientific thinker (which, interestingly enough, turns out in the end to be little if at all distinct from general intelligence). And his excellence in the one does not by any means prove to be a sign of great gifts in the other. Not only so, but even within the field of reproductive imagery, there are specific differences.

One person enjoys the most vivid visual pictures in his head; another has practically none, but can relive the varied experiences of sound. The visualiser will probably be able to draw from memory much better than he who cannot call up visual images; but the person with good auditory images will retain more of the content of oral lessons.

It is with regard to word-imagery that these differences have most importance in school work. It would seem to be true that some children learn to spell, for example, more easily if they write the words out several times; others, if they repeat the spelling verbally. As, however, we have not yet found any quick and easy ways of deciding this beforehand, these facts argue chiefly for a variety and a great elasticity of methods in teaching.

6. Backwardness in Reading

It will now, I think, be most useful if I take certain practical school subjects, and show how specific defects may enter into the work of a given child. Let me take reading as the first important example.

We meet children every day in nearly every school who are backward in reading, that is to say, who are a year or more behind the level of attainment normal for their age. Sometimes these children are retarded in everything else too, and these will commonly be children of low general mentality. But there are a number of cases where the backwardness is greater in reading than in any other subject, and here we at once suspect that some special disability is at work. When such children are examined in detail, a variety of causes will usually be found operative, some acting more powerfully with one child, some with another. It is very rarely that the difficulty can be attributed to one cause alone. And first of all the external factors of circumstance or school history must be ascertained.

These external factors in reading backwardness are themselves interesting and important. In some cases it is found that the child has had to change his school more than once just while he was first learning to read, and has got muddled and lost through this lack of continuity in teaching. In others, irregularity of attendance has meant broken teaching and the missing of essential steps. Physical defects such as poor eyesight, defective hearing, or some impediment in speech may have damaged the child's progress in the early stages of learning to read, and have left a permanent mark here, even though the defects have themselves been remedied later on. Again, lack of continuity between the methods of the Infants' School and those of the Primary School accounts for quite a large number of cases of backwardness in reading. This affects the weaker children the more powerfully. The gifted ones will have got past the early stages before such a change comes, but the laggards, with whom teaching methods make the most difference, may be just at a critical phase when this break occurs, and so lose their way. A closer cooperation between the departments might remedy this.

Too great a rigidity in following one particular mode of teaching may account for other cases. Some children undoubtedly learn best by one method, such as the word-whole method; others may get on best with the phonic method. And another influence that operates again most powerfully with the duller children is starting teaching too early, before the pupil has any effective interest in the subject. The highly intelligent child nearly always is spontaneously interested in learning to read, and very often has powerful motives deriving from home circumstances. But the child from a meaner home, or the child with a less mature mind, has no particular drive towards reading. And if he has no motive to help him get over the mechanical part, he will readily develop a dislike and fear of reading that will hamper his efforts still further. With the duller children it is of the first importance to awaken their interest in the subject, and to give them a lively sense of its value and the pleasure it may bring, before driving too hard at the mechanical side.

These external factors are of course all the more potent when they are allied with some specific defect in the particular mental processes involved in reading.

The innate defects are themselves of more than one sort, for reading is a highly complex accomplishment. It involves several different mental processes—the appreciation of visual word-wholes and their detailed parts, of sound-wholes and their parts; the co-ordination of complicated movements of mouth, lips, and tongue; the binding of all these elements together into a most intricate system of wholes and parts; and the linking up of all these mechanical symbols with their meanings in the understanding of what is read. Now the latter function is chiefly an affair of general intelligence. The bright child will have little difficulty here, although the duller child may find this his greatest stumbling-block. But the mechanics of reading will sometimes bother even the intelligent child, for it is there that special defects operate.

These special defects may be of the following kinds. A child may be poor in discriminating visual forms, so that he tends to mix up letters and words that are at all similar in shape. Or he may be weak in sound discrimination, finding it hard to distinguish between words nearly alike in sound, or to analyse the word as heard into its details. Again, it may not be so much a failure of actual perception when the word is seen or heard, but rather an inability to recall either the visual form or the sound of letters and words. Sometimes this is not a failure of immediate memory, but of remote. That is to say, the child may seem to be profiting from a lesson, but cannot retain what he has learnt for later recall. And, lastly, there seems to be in some cases a general language disability which cannot be put down to any of the previous causes, but denotes a failure to analyse and synthesise words and sentences, although general reasoning capacity and general ability may be normal. In such cases, however, one tends to suspect the presence of some powerful emotional factor, blocking the language function.

And how very important such emotional factors are is being more and more clearly established by those who are studying children backward in reading. Not a few cases of serious retardation in reading turn out to be due simply and solely to lack of confidence. Sometimes children who are quite unable to read at school, show themselves really able to do so under the hands of a skilled and sympathetic investigator, although not believing themselves in their own powers. Another striking piece of evidence which has emerged from the work of remedial teaching is the fact that very often when a psychologist has coached the child out of his special difficulties and brought him up to the level appropriate for his age, the child will again be "unable" to read when he returns to school. That is to say, the ability to read (like most other abilities) is not a merely mechanical function which one either has or has not, and which can be exercised irrespective of the total situation. With the growing child at any rate, the ability to read is always an ability (or failure) to read *here* and *now*, with *these* particular persons listening, and in *these* particular circumstances. The emotional setting is thus the essential key, rather than any particular mechanical defect. All this naturally underlines how important it is to handle sympathetically children who are slow in learning to read, and to go patiently and clearly enough to build up a sense of confidence.

7. Backwardness in Arithmetic

It will have been seen from what I said about specific disabilities in reading how important it is to find the actual cause of backwardness, so that appropriate remedial teaching may be given. Now let us look from the same point of view at the problem of backwardness in arithmetic.

Here again the problem turns out to be very complex, for the various operations of arithmetic employ many different mental processes, some of a high intellectual order, others of a more routine nature. And once again we find influences at work which spring from the conditions of the child's environment in home and school, alongside those which arise from the internal factors of his own intellectual and temperamental characteristics. Let us look first at the external factors.

Children who come from poor or inferior homes very often show a poor sense of number (as well as of space relations), due to the fact that they have not had the ample play with building bricks, with games of skill and counting games, and with all the varied forms of handwork in which size and quantity and shape matter, enjoyed by children in happier homes as a matter of course from an early age. Their interest in number has thus never been awakened, nor have they had the concrete experiences on which the understanding of number relations rests. Clearly one of the first things that the Nursery and Infants' Schools need to do is to make up for such a lack by encouraging free play with varied sorts of number and geometrical material. Formal work cannot take the place of this.

Moreover, children from homes where conditions are very hard—where the food and sleep are irregular or meagre, where the little girl has to mind the baby and the little boy to run errands—tend to show the effects of fatigue and ill-nourishment more readily in arithmetic than in other school subjects. Progress in arithmetic needs a close attention to lessons and unbroken effort in practice. And these are not possible for the ill-fed or weary child. Such a child cannot hold his mind to a longish sum, and if his thoughts wander or get blurred in the middle, he is lost. If he dreams for a moment and loses the thread when a critical step is being demonstrated, then all his further notions may be muddled and full of gaps.

As regards school life itself, change of school and frequent or prolonged absences make progress in arithmetic slow and uncertain, because they often mean that essential steps in learning have been missed out, and always mean irregular and insufficient practice. Another like cause is rapid promotion. A child who is generally able or specially gifted in language may be moved up on these grounds. But unless special care is taken, this may mean that his arithmetical teaching is not continuous and properly graded, and that he misses some essential stage. In any inquiry into backwardness in arithmetic, children are found who have a special weakness in some one process, very often subtraction or division. In such cases, the child's errors are nearly all of the same kind and constantly present; and the cause is commonly this of having missed a step at some critical point. Where other influences are chiefly to blame, errors tend to be more erratic.

Another thing that may affect children's work in arithmetic is the extent to which the school links up this subject with practical pursuits—handwork, geometry and geography, shopping and home life. The interests of children in the Primary School years are still intensely practical. Formal and theoretical problems find little response in their minds, but the actual issues of practical life are real and compelling. If children have the chance to use what they learn, they learn far more rapidly and surely.

Too much written work, again, very often confirms the backward child in slow and clumsy ways which hold him up still further. Number games, however, help both the younger and the slower children, not only because they set up a favourable attitude of mind, but also because they give plenty of practice in quick oral adding, subtracting, multiplying, and dividing.

To turn now to the child's own disabilities. A poor auditory memory for numbers is a serious handicap in mechanical arithmetic, and may hold up development even in an intelligent child. There have been some striking cases of backwardness due to this difficulty, and even a moderate degree of this defect may hamper a child all through his arithmetical work.

Then again, some children seem to have poor ability in forming associations with symbols, such as figures. And this enters into all the routine processes. Unless the child can carry out the simpler operations with ease and speed, he is hampered in getting a grasp of the more complex arithmetical relations.

Occasionally one meets a child who seems to be deficient in the capacity for appreciating number relations as such—just as one sees those who seem to have a special facility for it and delight in it from the earliest days.

These would seem to be the chief sorts of native intellectual disability in arithmetic. If a child suffers from any of them, he will not be able to learn as quickly and easily as his fellows in the early stages, and in arithmetic confusion breeds confusion. His lack of understanding will affect all his later work. Not even extra teaching and drill will help him unless these are adapted to his special sort of difficulty.

In arithmetic, too, perhaps more than anywhere else, children may get held back from emotional causes as well as from inherent intellectual defects. Some recent investigators, indeed, doubt whether these latter have any importance to speak of. They incline, rather, to believe that backwardness in arithmetic is (apart from cases of all-round lack of intelligence) practically always due to an *inhibition* of understanding, arising either (or both) from fear and lack of confidence, or from faulty teaching in the early stages.

The nervous or neurotic child cannot easily keep his mind on what the teacher is saying. His attention readily wanders in the middle of a sum, and the rest of his work may be wrong even though the first part was correct. He may forget that he was supposed to be subtracting, and start adding or multiplying. And if he thus seems careless and inattentive, and suffers disapproval, the whole subject may come under a cloud of shame and unhappiness for him. Many children get an intense dislike of arithmetic, and then cannot do justice to themselves in it. In all such cases, mistakes will be irregular and fitful, but very frequent. And such children commonly find the mechanical drill which seems so urgently called for unbearably dull and boring.

Now the remedy here obviously is to win the child's active interest by letting him use all that he learns in practical pursuits. If he gets a sense of the value of accuracy and speed in calculating for practical purposes that appeal to him, he will the more readily put up with the needed drudgery. And it is even more important to build up a sense of confidence by letting him work at his own pace, and win facility in the earlier processes before struggling with the harder. With such children self-teaching material in its various attractive modern forms is most helpful. When forced to measure himself against other children in class work, the delicate or neurotic child may be too frightened to do well. But if he is left alone with the subject for its own sake, and his direct interest in it is aroused, he may get along quite well.

Cross-classification of groups for arithmetical work, bringing together those children whose difficulties are of a similar kind, and individual material and teaching, are essential for overcoming uneven development and special handicaps in arithmetic.

I have emphasised the importance of *interest* in this field. But the factor of interest may very well account for a great many of our special gifts and our special lacks, as these are seen in school work and in ordinary life. Take, for instance, one of the few clearly established sex differences in ability, the difference between boys and girls in mechanical understanding. That the majority of boys are superior to the majority of girls in the understanding of machines and of mechanical relations is certain. It is, however, thought by many psychologists that this is not a strictly innate difference in ability, but rather one that develops chiefly as a result of the direction of their interests. And this difference in interest is itself partly the effect of suggestion and environmental pressure, although in part it does appear to be spontaneous and inherent. Boys love to pull things to pieces and see how their insides work. With girls this wish to see the insides of things and how their parts work is early inhibited by the need to nurse and cherish, to admire things as a whole, and particularly living things. They fight shy of pulling things to pieces, as a sort of cruelty. This very early determination of interest and impulse then sets the child's experiences in a certain direction, and builds up one sort of knowledge and skill rather than another. And on such a foundation, the specialised interests and abilities of later life are developed.

It is more than likely that the gift of language too is the fruit of an early direction of interest. One child delights in words and the fun of making them from a very early age, and later on, in the subtler forms of verbal expression that have no meaning for another. The other finds greater pleasure in what his hands can do, or in the discovery of facts in the world of things. Even among quite young children, there are those who are more interested in the physical world than in people, and others who take a dramatic interest in human relations more particularly. And by the time these children reach the Primary School, such individual trends of interest will already have begun to mark out paths of special knowledge and ability, leading one to excel in handwork, another in mathematics, a third in drama and literature, a fourth in song and rhythmic movement, a fifth in drawing and painting.

In these differences we touch upon the most profound problem of the mental life, that of the relation between understanding and purpose, between the activity of knowing and those of wishing and feeling.

But whether or not the psychologists can tell us how these differences in specific abilities and interests come about, as teachers we have to adapt ourselves to them if we want our children to reap the full benefit of their school life.

Chapter 3 · Social Development

1. Movement and Growth

In my discussion of the children we teach, I have so far spoken mainly of the differences between one child and another of the same age. Now I want to go on to their common characteristics, and to the *general* modes of behaviour which can be seen among children as they move through the age groups of the Primary School. When all allowances for the particular ways of particular children have been made, there still remain characteristic modes of thinking and feeling and doing of children in these years. And schools have of course to be planned in the large upon the needs of the general run of their pupils.

Now these general characteristics of the Primary School period will not be shown fully by any one child. No real living child is "typical" or "average". These notions are just useful tools to help us fix in our minds what there is in common between the actual children we observe. Some writers on psychology are fond of talking about *The Child*, almost as if there was a fixed real type that could in some mysterious way be distilled out from the actual children we know. And this leads to all sorts of rigid laws being laid down, and hard and fast notions of development being applied, which leave the practical person high and dry when he comes to deal with the living children in his class. For these reasons, I always try to anchor my own thought to the plural form, to talk of *children* rather than "the child", so as to remind myself constantly of the infinite variety of ways in which this, that, and the other child may depart from the general law.

Having here, however, already considered at length the fact of individual differences, I can now go on to draw the general outline of growth in these years, without misleading my readers.

The first general characteristic of Primary School children to be noted is their need for active movement. Left to themselves and given any chance at all, children of these years are well-nigh tireless in physical activity—running and jumping and climbing, skipping and playing with balls, using their hands to make and to explore, shouting and singing. I happen to live near one of the pleasantest open spaces of London, and in all out-of-school hours and holidays I hear the voices of children who have come to the green grass from the side streets round about, and I can look up to watch them swinging and leaping, playing cricket and football, chasing each other, making tents with a few rags and sticks, arguing and teasing. And I still hear them cheerfully shouting as their unwilling feet take them home at the latest hour of the evening.

And how they rush and run about the playground the moment they are released from the various pressures by which we keep them sitting quiet in the schoolroom! Always their natural impulses drive them *to be doing*, with hands and feet and tongue. This is their spontaneous way of taking the world, and their natural means of growth.

When we study their development in close detail by the experimental methods of the psychologist, we begin to find some of the reasons why children in these, no less than the Infants' School years, feel such a constant urge towards movement. Neither the development of their senses, nor the control and co-ordination of their muscles, is yet anything like complete. The acuity of vision, for example, is still improving all through the years from seven to eleven. Most important from the point of view of practical skill, the "muscle sense" (awareness of one's own movement through minute sense organs lying in the muscles, joints, and tendons) does not reach its finest sensitivity until twelve or thirteen years. The *speed* of adjusted movements, e.g. tapping or writing, shows a rapid increase from seven to ten years, after which the rate of improvement gradually slows down. And *accuracy* of movement improves markedly from five to nine years, and then rather less rapidly up to adolescence.

It is thus not only the children in the Infants' School who need opportunity for sense development and for practising bodily skill. Primary School children need it no less. They can do more things, and different things, but they have just as much need of actual bodily *doing*. Their muscles cry out for exercise, their senses for experience. And only by their own experience can they be educated. Bodily activity is not with children as with grown-ups a mere matter of taking enough exercise to keep healthy, nor of mere personal delight. It is these; but it is also a necessity of their education.

Without it they cannot attain full development of skill and power and sensitivity. Nor, as I shall show later on, can they enjoy the freest exercise of their understanding and reason.

The first great duty of the educator is thus to create such conditions as will allow the freest possible and the most ample bodily *movement*. When we ask children *not* to move, we should have excellent reasons for doing so. It is stillness we have to justify, not movement. There should be something real to be gained by it, some definite constructive end. Sitting still is a virtue only if it is a means to some purpose beyond itself. The end of education in these years is that the children should grow and develop, and to this, activity of one sort or another is the only key.

One point of the utmost practical importance is that not until about seven years of age is the co-ordination of the larger joints and muscles, e.g. hip, knee, and shoulder, thoroughly well established. Until that point is reached, however, the time is not yet ripe for the co-ordination of the smaller joints and muscles, fine movements of the fingers and wrist, delicate adjustments of the eyes, and even sensitive control of the mouth and larynx in speech and song. It is, of course, the Infants' School for which this fact has its greatest significance. Our methods there have even yet not taken enough account of it. We still start to teach accuracy in writing and drawing and needlework too early. We still make too big a demand on fine adjustments of hand and eye, instead of giving plenty of opportunity for the larger, more vigorous movements which lay a solid foundation for skill in the later years.

But happily the general current of change in Infants'
School methods is now moving steadily in the right
direction.

In the Primary School, these facts of development
also have great significance. We can legitimately call
for more accuracy and for finer work than in the
Infants' department. But we should not make this
demand suddenly, nor without gradation. Nor should
we even yet carry it too far. In these years too, plenty
of large free activity makes for sounder and fuller
development than niggling correctness of detail.

When we try to make a child read type that is too
small (and between the years eight and eleven, type
should not be less than 2 mm. in height), draw with too
fine a pencil, sew with too fine a needle and thread, and
do all these things with an accuracy appropriate to
years beyond his age, we tend to damage his eyesight,
strain his temper, and disturb his mental poise. We
can often get him to do these things successfully under
the subtle pressure of fear or ambition or the wish to
please us; but he has to pay the price. The increase in
serious defects of the eye which the statistics show in
the years after seven is one part of the price. Nervous
strain and loss of mental resilience are less plain but
not less potent.

In general, then, our attitude to children's movement
in the Primary School years should be to *use* it, not to
inhibit it.

We already make a good deal of wise provision for
the direct training of bodily activity, in drill and games
and rhythmic movement, as well as in the brief intervals
of free play. It is doubtful whether we go far enough

in this, however. The health and happiness of children (and their teachers!) would probably be much improved if the actual time given to physical exercise in the open air were increased. Illnesses due to lack of air and sun and exercise are the commonest type of sickness in children between seven and eleven years.

But the problem is not just one of sandwiching periods of physical activity in between periods of immobile "headwork". The headwork itself is most fruitful when it is also handwork and bodywork. In these years, the child's intelligence is essentially practical. He thinks as much with his hands as with his tongue; and even with his tongue he can think better aloud than "in his head".

The whole of his education needs to be conceived in terms of his own activity. His desire for movement is part of his desire for expression and for understanding. His delight in rhythm and pattern, in music and dancing, in miming and making things, no less than his love of running and jumping and playing games, show how urgent and how educative his impulse to movement is. We must meet this need by giving him ample experience in the arts and crafts as well as in games and drill.

Even this, however, does not exhaust our practical opportunities for making use of the child's desire for activity. The whole physical setting of the school and classroom should be based upon the creative value of the child's own movements. The furniture and equipment will help or hinder just as readily as our explicit methods of teaching. There is no real place in the Primary School, any more than in the Infants'

School, for heavy fixed desks and inaccessible store
cupboards. Light movable tables and chairs, individual
material arranged so that the children can get it themselves and be individually responsible for keeping it in
order, a discipline and a classroom organisation built
upon the active sharing of work and play, all make for
social control as well as for bodily poise.

I want now to discuss those broad facts of social
development in young children which underlie this
view that classroom organisation should be based
upon movement rather than upon stillness.

2. Social Life in the Infants' School

One of the most marked differences between children
under seven and those of eleven and over lies in their
social behaviour. For example, the Infants' School
child still clings closely to parent or teacher, and he
lets us see most of his feelings quite vividly. His brother
who is about to leave the Primary School is far more
independent of all the world of grown-ups, and far
more reserved in expressing his emotions.

These changes are not only very interesting in
themselves. They are of great importance for our ways
of handling children at different ages. The child of
eleven is open to different appeals and has different
standards of behaviour from those of the seven-year-
old. The question of discipline and social life in the
Primary School cannot easily be dealt with as a single
problem, for these years do not form a single period
showing the same sort of social responses throughout.
Critical changes are going on in the earlier part of the

period, say from seven to eight. Then there comes a time of comparatively slow but steady development, up to about twelve years of age, when in its turn the new ferment of adolescence begins. The characteristics of nine to twelve years are well enough marked, and might be said to give us the typical picture of the Primary School child. But it is important to remember that the children in the lower groups are still in an age of more rapid psychological changes, continuous with the Infants' School period.

We can see most clearly what the lines of social development are in the Primary School years if we first look briefly at the behaviour of children in the Infants' School, and then follow the changes through. And it is wise to observe the children's behaviour, not only in the situations organised by us in classroom and home, but also in their spontaneous play with each other when no adults are interfering. It is here that they reveal their inner minds naïvely and freely, offering us new light upon their conduct in home and school.

One of the first things to be remarked is that children's social development and their intellectual growth are very intimately connected at every age. It is hardly possible to say that either is *determined* by the other. By special pleading, a case might be made out to show that children's growth in understanding fixes their type of social behaviour at any age. For example, it could be said with some truth that a child's behaviour in the earlier years was bound to be determined simply by personal fears and affections, not by moral ideals, since his mind cannot yet grasp abstract notions of good and evil. What is "naughty" means for the little child simply and literally "what makes grown-ups angry". It is only when in adolescence he begins to be able to think in terms of abstract *ideas* that he can begin to be moved by impersonal *ideals*. And the mentally defective child, whose intellectual growth never reaches the level of abstract thought, is all his life moved only by simple pains and pleasure.

But so far are we in fact from being able to say that the growth of understanding is the *cause* of social development, that it is now possible for Piaget, one of the ablest observers of children, to argue the very reverse. He wants to put almost the whole responsibility for intellectual advance upon the stimulus of social experience. On his view, it is *because* the child becomes much more sensitive to the opinions of others and less self-centred that at about seven or eight years of age he starts out on the path from the simple direct seeing and handling of the world to thinking in abstract terms and to reflecting upon thought itself and so making it orderly.

On my view, however, it is more just and more repaying to take neither of these two fixed positions. It is better not to try to say of intellectual and social growth which is cause and which effect, but rather to look upon the child's development, with all its varied aspects, as a single whole at every age. Every sort of change is bound up with every other. For our own convenience in study, we may pick out now one, now another of the aspects of growth, but they are never separate in fact. Nor can we ever say that one dominates the rest. It is always the whole child who plays and laughs, who quarrels and loves, who thinks and asks questions, through all the hours of his day and all the years of his childhood.

If then at any point in this discussion I emphasise the importance of understanding as a factor in social life, or at another of the value of social contacts as a spur to thought, I should like my readers to remember that what I most want to do is to show the *mutual* influence of thought and behaviour throughout.

Let us now look at the broad characteristics of the social behaviour of children in the later years of the Infants' School, as a starting-point for the study of their development in the Primary School.

As every Infants' School teacher knows, children under seven are very dependent upon the smiles or the frowns of adults. The approval or disapproval of the grown-up in charge is on the whole much more significant to little children than the opinions or wishes of their fellows. The boys and girls in an infants' class will be separately friendly or defiant to the teacher. They do affect each other to some extent, of course, and sometimes waves of restlessness or of giggles will run through the whole room. But the children rarely band together in steady hard defiance of the teacher, as children of ten and eleven may do. Nor is it easy to build up a true and continuous group spirit of order and effort amongst them. The teacher's relation remains almost entirely personal and direct with each child. A clever teacher can of course create real co-operation among six- and seven-year-olds, in games, in song and dance, and in group handwork; but to keep this alive needs constant inspiration and active suggestion from her. The fears and affections of children under seven are thus mainly orientated to the grown-up, that is, to parents and those who take over the function of parents.

In the playground or the play-hour at home, little children do form themselves into spontaneous groups for this or that game. These groups are, however, quite unstable, and liable to break down at any moment through rivalry or a quarrel about some belonging, or through the wish to join another group which suddenly becomes more attractive. They are quite different from the close corporations and stable "gangs" to be seen among children of ten to twelve. They are in fact hardly "groups" at all in the psychological sense, but rather temporary alliances for the purpose of individual play.

The child in the Infants' School is still almost entirely an individualist. His world is very largely centred in his own feelings. He cannot take the point of view of others, since his own needs and wishes are too urgent. Even when he is playing with others, he is more occupied with his own phantasies than with the wishes or ideas of other children. Each child in such a group can be seen using the others for his own purposes, and if their wishes happen to fit in, all goes well. But if the will of any child in the group cuts across the interests of the others, squabbles soon break out. If one child wants to be the "captain" and the others are content to be his "soldiers", everything goes happily. But if the "soldiers" tire of being ordered about and want to take the lead in their turn, the first "captain" may easily refuse to play any longer. If one girl's desire to play the "mother" and take care of her family of "babies" finds a response in the mood of her companions, and they are content to be nursed and fed and scolded, then the group remains a single whole of happy players. But should one of the "babies" conceive the ambition to change roles with the "mother", the whole thing may break up into tears and quarrels, or change into a quite new game. It might well be said that the child of, say, five years, typically plays in the presence of others, or uses them as pawns in his own game, rather than plays *with* them in any co-operative sense. The group is little more than a background for each child's individual activities.

Even at seven years of age, this picture is still largely true. The child of seven has certainly begun to play *with* others, although not yet in the sense in which the young footballer of ten or twelve plays with (and for) his team. He is still chiefly concerned to show off his own prowess, and is hardly yet beginning to be able to feel himself one with others, part of a whole larger than himself.

Yet the signs of change are there. Groups formed spontaneously in play are more stable and lasting than earlier, and hint at the beginnings of the true "team-spirit". In the classroom it is becoming a little easier to weld the scholars together into a more permanent whole, and the children are beginning to be able to see things sometimes from the point of view of others.

3. Children's Ideals and Notions of Punishments

The fact that young children's minds are mostly orientated towards parents and teachers rather than towards others of their own age, is at the root of another very striking characteristic of social life in these early years. If we watch children under seven when they are playing their favourite games of dramatic make-believe, and listen to what is said by the make-believe father and mother to their babies, the captain to his men, the railway guard to his passengers, indeed, any person of power and authority to his subordinates, we shall notice that these make-believe authorities are all most tyrannical in their demands and severe in their punishments and penalties. They are usually far more so than the real persons in real life, or than anything the children themselves have actually experienced.

One might perhaps have expected that where we see the "pretend" mothers and teachers being very strict with their play-children, the little players have themselves been severely treated in real life. And sometimes of course this is the case. But it is by no means always so. I have known children from the most liberal homes and with the mildest and most gentle parents, children who have hardly ever been scolded let alone punished, behave towards their make-believe families and pupils with the greatest severity.

As an instance, one small boy of five years, whom I observed in his spontaneous play with other gently nurtured children, had been brought up in a home where the theories of education adopted did not allow the use of such words as "naughty", nor of scoldings and punishments. Yet he would join with his playmates in the most emphatic use of such words to his make-believe children of the moment. One of his friends, a girl who had a mother of the most tolerant temperament and who was used to a mild rule both at home and in school, would sometimes take a younger child in the family play and shake her, saying in the severest tones, "You *naughty* child! You bad wicked baby!" When she was seven, this same child would sometimes say of one of her family of dolls, "May has been a horrid little beast, and I'll have to give her a good whipping!"

The same sort of thing can be seen with any group of young children playing freely together in homes and gardens, or in the parks and the streets, whatever sort of upbringing they have had. The details will vary a little with differences in the children's temperament, but we can safely say that in this respect children's play behaviour has very little to do with their real experiences. It is rather an expression of what is going on in their own minds at this stage of development.

In their real relations with other children, too, young children are often far harder on each other than the grown-ups would ever be. Children of, say, six or seven years will judge the behaviour or the achievements of their fellows, and particularly of those a little younger or weaker than themselves, far more harshly than parent or teacher would. Let them comment freely upon each other's work, and you will hear such remarks as "John can't draw engines." "That's a silly picture." "We don't like Tommy, he shouts so." "Fred says 'likkle' instead of 'little'—isn't he stupid?" "Albert is a dirty boy—now we *don't* like him." And if one child should cry when he tumbles, the others are often ready to scorn his weakness and say, "He's a *baby*!" This does not always happen, of course. They are often tender and protective to the smaller and

weaker ones, too. But when they are feeling critical of
the younger or less skilful, they are far more severe
than we should want to be. They cannot temper their
judgments nor keep them in proportion. They cannot
make allowances. They must always be *either* wholly
admiring or wholly contemptuous. It is the grown-up
in charge who has to keep the balance, to encourage the
weaker ones, and to try to educate the superior children
towards a more just and temperate judgment of
others.

In the home, too, children of six to eight will often
try to rule the comings and goings of younger brothers
and sisters with a real tyranny, deciding which toys
they are to play with, how they are to use their
toys, when they are to be put away, and in general, acting out the part of the strictest parents. On the least
opening, in fact, children of these years will assume the
rôle of parent (or teacher) to other children. The relation
of parent and child, rather than that of brother and
sister comrades, dominates both their inner life and
its natural outward expression. I shall show later on
how this picture changes, and how in the later Primary
School period children turn to other children as their
natural *allies* against authority.

Now if we ask why this should be so, why for instance
young children are so hard on each other's achievements and judge with so harsh a standard, the answer
is that in so doing they are supporting *themselves* against
the "babyishness", the tears, the clumsiness, the lack
of control upon which they turn so severe an eye in
others. As with us grown-ups too, they castigate in
others the very faults they are struggling against in

themselves. They can only dare to be mild and tolerant of the weaknesses of others when their own impulses of anger and fear are more firmly leashed, and their own skills more securely won.

In his experimental studies of social development in children (to be described in his next volume, now being translated), Piaget also has found characteristic attitudes in the younger children which conform with the facts I have observed in their spontaneous play. In some very interesting experiments, he studied the attitude of children of different ages to *rules*. For instance, he played the game of marbles with one child after another, getting the child to explain the rules to him, and asking searching questions about the rules so as to bring out what the child thought about them. Then in playing he would break one of the rules in order to find what the child's notions about this would be. And he found that the attitude of children under seven or eight was in many ways very different from that of children of ten to eleven years.

Children under seven or eight, for example, believe that rules are *absolute* things. They are not, as to us and to older children, mere conventions agreed upon by the players of the game. They are things which have existed from time immemorial, and if made, then made by God or by great human figures in an ancestral past. They are not to be questioned, nor can they be altered. Thus they have a sacrosanct quality—indeed the young child does not distinguish between the rules of games and moral laws. All these things are absolute commands, never to be changed and never (in theory) to be broken. If they were disobeyed, then the punishment would be dire. Anything might happen, and nothing would be too severe to be just.

Piaget studies also the ideas of children about punishments appropriate to such a sin as lying. He told each child a story about a boy who lied to his mother, and suggested certain punishments, ranging from mild and sensible penalties to really harsh punishments. And he found that the younger children always deemed the harshest punishment to be the only one suitable—whereas the older children held the milder penalty to be more just. The younger ones have little or no sense of proportion and no tolerance.

How faulty this sense of proportion is was shown to me one day by a little girl who, after her first day at a nursery school, asked her mother, "Mummy, what would happen if children were naughty in school?" Her mother wisely wanted to know what was in the child's own mind, and so asked in her turn, "Well, what do you think might happen?" "God would drown the world," the child replied.

The results of all these observations and experiments, moreover, fit in with what is being revealed of the deeper minds of little children by the methods of psycho-analysis. In their imagination, young children do really fear the direst penalties for their naughtinesses and even for their very wishes. Their notions of justice and of what their parents may do to them are built upon the pattern of their own surging wishes and angers and fears, and are as little measured. They cannot yet test their phantasies by their experience of reality, since this is as yet so meagre and limited.

And of course it is the older children with a more

tempered awe of the rules of a game who are in fact more able to keep the rules. The younger children, unable to tolerate the *idea* of altering or disregarding rules, do in reality transgress them far more frequently. Piaget found that a younger child who thought cheating a most terrible crime might yet cheat in fact, and while doing it, cheat *himself* too into believing that he had nevertheless really won the game. Whereas the boy of ten or twelve, more matter of fact in his notions, not imagining that the sky would fall down if he did cheat, would yet rather more easily resist the temptation to do it. For most children of these older years, a game won by cheating or by breaking the rules would hardly be won at all.

Here we see, then, one of the big differences between the Infants' School and the Primary School child. The moral values and the social judgments of the older child are, on the one hand, more temperate and more sensible than those of the younger; and on the other hand, they are distinctly more effective and reliable in reality.

4. Loving and Hating

In speaking of the naïve egoism of children under seven, I noted the fact that children of these years do often form spontaneous groups for make-believe play and games, but I went on to say that these groups are always very unstable and evanescent. Now I want to follow out more closely the reasons for this, as they throw light on the typical course of social development in the later Primary School years.

People sometimes talk as if young children were individualists because of something yet *lacking*, because, for example, the so-called "social instincts" have not yet begun to develop. But close observation shows that it is not really that the children are *short* of certain definite instincts appearing later on. It is much more truly that their first impulses towards each other go through certain changes in mode of expression with the children's growth and added experience. These changes are continuous throughout development, although the end may appear very different from the beginning.

The group relations of children under seven are unstable, not because their goodwill for each other is weak, but because their hostility is equally strong. Their affections and admirations may be very warm and generous; but their jealousies and rivalries are warm and passionate too. That is the real difficulty in their social relations. They love and they hate with an equal simplicity and wholeheartedness, and they may pass in a moment from fondness to anger, from co-operation to quarrels and tears. They have not yet learnt to select their impulses along the lines of congenial friendships and settled loyalties.

Now if one watches a number of children of these years playing freely together, or listens to their talk about each other in their freer moments in classroom or corridor, one finds that they have a spontaneous solution for this ever-present conflict of friendship and rivalry. The friends within a group turn their hostility on to *outsiders*. They find *enemies* to dislike, and so are able to keep their love for their friends unblemished.

The spontaneity and dramatic vividness of this social mechanism is very striking. In one community of children under eight years of age I have watched its happening again and again. These were well-nurtured and well-trained children from very good homes, attending my own school. In their life within the school, these children were allowed more *verbal* liberty than is usual, although of course they were restrained from unkind actions, and we brought constant educational influences to bear to lead them towards mutual consideration and co-operation. My records of their behaviour in play, however, illustrate very clearly this reciprocal relation between loving and hating.

A group of playmates would often band together in expressing in the most dramatic way their momentary dislike for another child or a rival group. "Shall we bury Tommy in our castle?" "Shall we kill Bobbie?" "Shut John out. He's not coming with *us*." "There aren't any Marys in *our* train." "We hate Mark." "Dan's horrid." One child was fond of running round the room chanting, apropos of other children not at the moment approved by his particular group, "Wretched little Chris, wretched little Chris." Or two rival groups would battle with words, threatening to put each other "in prison". The elder boys sometimes really tried to shut one or two of the younger into a hut as a "prison". At one time it became the fashion to draw huge chalk "crocodiles" on the schoolroom floor (much used for drawing), with open mouths and large teeth, the artists threatening their enemies of the day that this would "bite your legs off". At another period, one little girl was often used as a foil to the loyalty of a certain group.

They would make hostile remarks such as "Oh look! There's that dragon." "The dragon has come!" Most of this was quite good-humoured, and the adults in charge saw to it that it remained so. But it was quite clear that if they had been left to themselves, the children would have carried this group rivalry to more determined lengths.

When a child was excluded from a particular group, he might want to be accepted back into it. And one of the ways of trying to make himself acceptable again would be to try to centre the hostility on another child, playing to the gallery in the most amusing way. For instance, a girl, Priscilla, and a boy, Chris, were on one afternoon rather hostile to another boy, Dan, who was normally their chief playmate. Priscilla was helping to dry all the children's legs after paddling, and said that "now" she wouldn't "do Dan". Dan said, "But I *must* be done, because I'm going out to tea," and made a long expostulatory monologue about it. Priscilla and Chris laughed, and said scornfully that "Dan doesn't know what he's talking about." Dan stamped his foot and said, "Yes, I *do*. But I'll tell you who does not know what he's talking about. *Mark* does not!" "Oh, yes, he does." Dan then put a pile of mud on the pathway, telling the other two that this was "so that Mark should slip on it when he ran". This was clearly in order to enlist the co-hostility of Priscilla and Chris against Mark, and so turn it from himself—although Mark again was ordinarily a particular friend of Dan's.

Now it was very plain that when their hostile feelings were thus turned towards outsiders, the members of any group loved, admired, "adored", followed or protected their fellows with all the greater fullness and stability.

Such a situation is of course not seldom seen in older children and grown-ups too. To turn our jealousies and rivalries outward, away from our own group, on to an outsider or "foreigner", has ever been one of the simplest ways of dealing with them, even for adults. The most impressive example is the way in which the flame of patriotism burns so much more brightly when men's hearts are drained of hatred and aggression towards their own countrymen by the national enemy. Those who lived through the early days of the Great War know the truth of this. But the same thing can be seen in class differences, in the struggles of political parties, in racial conflict, in the loyalties of town and village, and in the rivalries of sport.

In young children, however, this relation between loving and hating may be seen in its most naïve and spontaneous form. Since loyalties and rivalries are as yet fluid and unorganised, they show this social mechanism free from sophistication.

What happens to this tendency, in children over seven or eight years? The course of its later history can be understood from those facts of adult life just noticed. The quick-changing feelings of love and hostility which young children show for their play-mates settle slowly down into the more stable friend-ships and personal rivalries in the work and the games of later childhood. And the spontaneous animosities of early group relations are gradually taken up into the approved and organised rivalries of class or school, of team or club. We ourselves, as educators, make use of these rivalries for sustaining effort and building up the pride of achievement in work and in play.

The main line of change in the Primary School years is thus that these fleeting impulses of early childhood become gradually *organised*. They grow into more stable habits of feeling and doing, centred round more lasting groups associated for more settled and approved interests.

It is, of course, our convention to dwell rather upon the positive than on the negative aspects of rivalry. We speak in glowing terms of the values of loyalty within a group, and rather tend to slur over the enmity to opposing groups. Whether in sport or in scholarship, we praise the winning of the shield or cup by *this* group rather than scorn its losing by *that*. And this is profound educational sense. It is the right practical attitude. But when, as here, our aim is to *understand* what we act upon, we must look all the facts in the face. There cannot be any doubt that in the years of childhood and youth, brotherly love and co-operation with one's immediate fellows is fostered and supported by a healthy rivalry with other groups. Hard as it may be for adults to embrace all mankind within their love, such a catholic aim is out of reach for the child.

The compensating value of the rivalry of groups is that it brings to the children the active *experience* of mutual kindness and help within the group. They get the feel of working and playing *together*. They suffer the pressure of other children's wishes and contrary opinions which are yet not *too* different, not altogether contrary, since they come from friends. Each child's fondness for his fellow-members makes him more ready to give way, to try to see their point of view. It is possible to "give and take" with those whom one loves, although not with those whom one fears and dislikes.

It is, then, these loyalties to his immediate allies in the years from seven to eleven that make the bridge which carries the child over from his early self-seeking and self-centredness to the true social outlook which comes with the wider vision of adolescence. Our ultimate educational aim may be (and for myself I would say *must* be) to transcend all rivalries in national and international life. But to gain it, our children need the actual experience of the smaller units of social life that lie within the compass of their sympathy and their understanding.

5. Chums and Heroes

It is, first, this discovery of other children as *allies* which brings to children of the later Primary School years that characteristic reserve towards adults, and comparative independence of adult values, which make so great a contrast with children in the Infants' School.

Active comradeship with playmates and classmates brings the child support in two further directions: (*a*) against the hitherto dominating influence of the grown-ups, and (*b*) against the inner world of phantasy, so powerful in those earlier years.

In the years between seven and eleven, the adult is to a far smaller extent than before the immediate arbiter of the child's happiness. The child no longer hangs upon the grown-up's smiles and frowns with the helplessness of the Infants' School age. He is much more sensitive now to the praise or contempt of his chums. Giving away their secrets or becoming a "sneak-thief" will cause him more pangs of shame than defying a teacher—or even telling him a lie. And any band of playmates will in these years have many "secrets" into which they will not readily let a grown-up enter. This is the age of secret languages, those invented idioms and symbols, the idea of which seems to come quite spontaneously to many children. (Perhaps more often to girls than to boys, as boys run more readily to secret *deeds*.) Very often the sole purpose of such a private language will be to give the children using it the delicious sense of having a world all of their own, and being able to keep the grown-ups at bay. It may then be nothing but a few bits of gibberish, used mostly when grown-ups are about, just to tantalise them. Sometimes, however, it will be a full system of signs or words, used for telling stories or playing some elaborate game. This impulse to a secret code for use among themselves is very indicative of the attitude of children of these ages to grown-ups.

It is under the shelter of this alliance with others of his own age that the child wins his first real independence of his parents and teachers, and begins to see them more nearly as they are. They cease to be the gods, the giants and ogres that they were to his infantile imagination. He and his fellows together can now dare to look at the grown-ups with an appraising eye, and see whether they are indeed worthy of that respect which they demand. Children watch the behaviour of parents and teachers with quite as observant a glance as parents and teachers turn upon them, and often reflect upon what they see in a way that might disconcert most of us did we know it. Rasmussen quotes his elder girl, then nine years and four months, as saying of two of her school teachers: "We are good both in Miss X's and Miss Y's lessons. When Miss X goes out of the class-room, she always says: 'Now we shall see how good you can be while I am away'; and when she comes back she asks one of us if we have been good. But Miss Y never says anything special; there's more art in that."[1]

A nine-year-old friend of mine, after listening to her headmaster declaiming the verse of a certain poet with over-much emotion, commented with scorn—"He's just *silly*."

I have, for that matter, known children very much younger than nine years observe and reflect acutely upon the behaviour of grown-ups. Ursula, for example, when well under five, came home from her nursery school one day and told her mother, "Mummy, Miss J. says we can't have those sewing cards" (the old-fashioned Kindergarten sewing cards with small holes), " 'cos they're bad for our eyes. But Mummy, if they are, why did she let us have them last year?"

Ursula was an exceptionally intelligent child, encouraged to think and discuss freely. But what an unusual child in an unusual environment might do at five, the ordinary child begins to do as a matter of normal everyday development, in the years of the Primary School. (Daisy Ashford was nine when she wrote *The Young Visiters*.) Neither teacher nor parent can now maintain his prestige by mere virtue of being grown-up. Authority has to be won and kept by the

[1] V. Rasmussen, *The Primary School Child*, p. 79.

real tested qualities of sense and firmness. And any Primary School child worth his salt will be continually trying out the power of the adult to keep his allegiance, as many of us may even know to our cost! He will be quick to sense and despise weakness, and quite merciless to exploit it. But he will be as ready to yield respect to those grown-ups who are at the same time tolerant, good-humoured, and sure of themselves.

He will be excellent friends with us when we deserve it. And yet he will never take us into the kingdom of his inner mind, as the young child does, and as the adolescent boy and girl will do in their turn. He has less intimate need of *us* in these years, and far more of his mates. If we play the part of sensible, decent, friendly, perhaps remote but entirely human elders, free from humbug, from tyranny and from any fear of him, he will be content with us.

This need of Primary School children for authority that is genuine, though mild and understanding, is bound up with the general movement of their minds towards reality and away from phantasy. They begin to want real achievement, real skill, in every direction. As they leave the Infants' School years farther behind, their feet are even in their dreams planted more firmly on the solid earth, and they seek fulfilment there. Jack no longer dreams of destroying the Ogre of the Beanstalk, but of hunting elephants and braving hostile Indians. After the age of eight years, fairy-tales give place in children's reading to stories of animals, and of exploits in far lands. This is of course more true of boys than of girls, with whom the interest in fairy-tales lasts rather longer. But girls too begin to love stories of real animals, preferring, however, to read of the dogs and cats of the domestic hearth than of the animals of the wild. Folk-lore, myth, and legend still hold an interest; but these have almost as much *convention* about them as the novel and drama of a later age, and do not wear that air of their own reality which belongs to the fairy-tale and the make-believe of infancy.

I shall take up again for their own sake the changes in the reading interests of children as they grow through the Primary School period. At the moment, I am using these facts just to illustrate my general point of the child's increasing wish for real activity and real success. And the same trend of development can be shown if we look at their spontaneous expressions of phantasy in original writings. I have before me a school magazine made up of stories and poems all written by a group of boys between eight and nine years of age. They make very clear the way in which children's minds at this age move away from the world of giants and trolls and witches and magic carpets to something more nearly resembling the everyday world of reality.

Here are the *Adventures* of one of our young writers: "I was in bed when I had an exciting dream and this is what it was. I was in a field when out of the corner of my eye I saw a club fall. I tried to dodge it but too late. All was blank. When I recovered I found I was in a cell bound and gagged. I struggled and strained but all in vain. In my struggles I had got upright. It was then that I saw a glimmer of light high up. I managed to get up on a stool and I found there was a window. I stood on tip toe and knocked it down with my head. Some glass fell down and I got down from the stool and found a suitable piece of glass to cut the cords. When I had got free I looked for the door. I could not find it so I climbed through the window and escaped."

And here is a melodrama of everyday life: *The Villain*. "Once when I was asleep I dreamed a dream that I was out with somebody and we went in to a tube train. There was a girl friend of mine there and she told me that her father was a murderer. She pointed to a man in the train. Then I saw the man take a knife out of one of his pockets and open the blade, and put the knife to a man's heart, and he stabbed him. There lay the man dead. Then the villain walked over to me, and put the knife to my heart and was just going to stab me, when I grabbed the knife and shut up the blade. The train stopped so my friend and me got out. I ran along to a policeman, who was on the platform. I gave him the knife and he said 'Now come along to the villain.' We found the villain and he was taken to prison."

These heroisms are not altogether out of the reach of the young authors—if only they were a little bigger and stronger! And these villains might well be met with any day!

In the Primary School Report, it is said that all witnesses agreed that Primary School children are very matter-of-fact. Here is a poem from an eight-year-old which bears this out.

BED

I love to be in bed,
With a pillow at my head,
And a lovely book to read,
With lovely food to eat,
And a bottle at my feet.

That matter-of-factness is itself but an expression of the effort of the child of this age to lay hold of real things, to encompass the world of phantasy with real achievement.

6. The Need for Activity

Let me now summarise briefly the contrasts already noted between the social development of children in the Infants' School and in the Primary School, remembering, of course, that the differences are never absolute, but always a matter of less or more.

The Infants' School child is self-centred and egoistic. Other children are chiefly looked upon as rivals for the love of grown-ups or the ownership of playthings. They may be warmly loved, but love may break down at any moment through the force of rivalry. Children may play together, but only for naïvely selfish ends, and do not yet form stable groups. The grown-ups have far more influence over the child's happiness or misery than his playmates, and he will betray the latter at any moment for the favour of the former. From the grown-up he seeks tenderness and protection, and he fears the most severe punishments for trifling naughtiness. He lives far more fully in the world of make-believe than in that of cold reality.

The typical child of eight to eleven years has become much less naïvely self-centred. He can now play and work with others more sustainedly, and prefers this to playing alone. Other children (or at any rate some of them) have become allies, and his friendships are far more stable. His rivalries have settled down into orthodox patterns in games and sports, and he is, towards the end of the period, beginning to think of himself as a part of this or that social whole. He is now less moved by the comments of parent or teacher than by the praise or blame of his chums. He is reserved with grown-ups, although he appreciates their "decency" and respects real authority. He prefers organised games with definite rules and arrangements to "go as you please" individual play. He is matter-of-fact in his ambitions and day-dreams, and anxious to gain real skill and to do real things. He is more sensible and tolerant in his moral judgments, and somewhat scornful and suspicious of sentiment.

He is not yet capable of truly disinterested effort, nor can he follow ideal ends unless they are firmly anchored to people and things he knows and understands. He delights in trials of individual skill and ingenuity. Even when he plays and works with others, he does so mainly for his own glory. The "team-spirit" is foreshadowed but not yet realised. The habit of playing with others, and the actual experiences of social give-and-take, are laying the foundations of more disinterested social purpose during these years.

And this is where we come to practical considerations. For whether or not these foundations of later social life are well laid depends in large measure upon what happens to the child now.

The natural phases of development we have been studying certainly fix the broad limits of the child's growth at any age. But these limits *are* very broad, and leave a great deal of room for education. They determine the possibilities, but not the actualities. To realise vividly what a difference actual experience may make, we have but to compare the "only" child kept in the nursery until eight or nine with boys and girls of the same age who have enjoyed a full life with others in a large family or a good school; we have but to contrast the children of a school where every movement is frowned upon and every enterprise stifled, with those of another that encourages active effort and values independence.

No method of education will give to the child of the Infants' School the *camaraderie* of the older schoolboy, or endow the youngster of eleven with the vision and virtues of eighteen. But it is equally certain that if the infant is allowed to enjoy life fully *as* an infant, finding free expression for his phantasies and gaining skill and knowledge according to his measure, he will be all the healthier and more sensible as a Primary School boy. And if boys and girls of the Primary School years have the chance to play and to work in real active relationships with their fellows, exercising every social gift within their scope, the wider social aims and more disinterested ideals of adolescence will come to fuller fruition and be more securely based.

That is why it is useful to study first what the natural directions of growth are. Only so can we know the special needs of the child at this or that age, and what demands we can wisely make upon him.

Take, for instance, that question of his not wanting to "split" on his comrades. His schoolmaster wants information about a certain happening. He is sure certain boys know. Ought he to make one of them, through fear or bribery, "tell on" the others? In this not uncommon situation, there is a genuine clash of values. The boys are aligned as a group against the master as a person, against the larger world of "the school". He may appeal to them on the ground of some remote and abstract ideal, but they cannot detach that from him. The master might feel impelled to break down their loyalty to their friends—but would this really be desirable? There may be circumstances in which it has to be done, but in general there can be little doubt that it is a far greater help to children's social development if we ourselves respect their mutual loyalties. The return is often a hundred fold, in trust and confidence in us, and in real growth towards those larger allegiances we are aiming at.

In the social life of the Primary School we have to cut our coat according to our cloth. We must not expect the far-seeingness or the self-control of a later age. Children of these years are not ready for "self-government" in any large sense. To offer it would be putting upon them a greater responsibility than they can bear. They cannot yet understand complex social relationships, nor does their vision carry them much beyond the immediate situation.

But within the limits of their understanding and control, they *can* wield genuine responsibility. And they need to have the opportunity. Keeping them quiet in their desks while we lecture to them about possible virtues will not carry them out of the egoism of childhood. Having a limited but definite and active share in the care of the classroom, the handwork material, the book cupboard, the school garden, and animal pets, will beyond doubt help to do so. The Primary School still has much to learn here from Montessori or Kindergarten customs. Far more social use might be made of the tidying and repairing and decorating of the schoolroom walls and furniture and equipment than is usually done. The wall surfaces, for instance, usually leave little room for decoration, and what there is is commonly filled by miscellaneous pictures of the grown-ups' choice. What a waste of possibilities in active co-operative effort—not to mention æsthetic training! And children of these years delight in painting and designing and making curtains and boxes and shelves, for the use of each and the pleasure of all.

The value for *social* education of all the arts and handicrafts, when taught with practical sense and adapted to real needs, is very great. Children will not learn co-operation, needless to say, through formal lessons or through handicrafts mechanically taught. There is no social education for a class of forty children in all making the same paper or cardboard or wood model at the same time. There *is* such an education when the end is a common one and the making is shared, each having his own individual contribution which may differ from everyone else's and yet help to create the whole—especially if the whole be needed for a definite purpose—a series of maps, a wall design, a cooked meal, an illustrated class magazine, a set of boxes to keep material in, the costumes and scenery for a play. Crude and simple these things will have to be, but they can be done and bring much delight in the doing.

The social values of games and sports is now, too, becoming more widely realised. To learn to take turns in the chance of jumping farther, running faster, climbing higher, and throwing a ball better, than anyone else, learning to fail as well as to succeed, to play with others as well as against them, to be a leader one day and a follower the next, these offer rich food for social growth. Such experiences get taken up into the very stuff of the child's nature in a way that no fine sermons of ours can ever be. And they build step by step on what can actually be achieved by the child in each year of his development.

No less is the social value of song and dance and drama. The dance and the drama are social in their very origin, bound up with the ancient communal rites of life and death. And every time children do these things together, they are carried by so much out of the circle of their naïve egoism by that very sense of *togetherness* which cannot be taught nor learnt except through being experienced.

The modern stress on individual work and individual progress, so necessary in the formal subjects, finds its corrective in these activities that are social and communal from their very nature. Yet even here we should not strive too hard for unselfishness, nor try to force the "team-spirit" prematurely. If we do, we may stultify their growth. Let the child frankly enjoy his pride in his own prowess, whilst these actual situations of doing and making and playing and singing and dancing together with others are fertilising his spirit as they will. The seed will ripen in its own time, if we but sow it. It is inactivity that is barren.

Chapter Four · Intellectual Development

1. The Child's Need to Understand

In the last chapter, I tried to make plain some of the reasons why an education planned in terms of the children's own activity is so much more fruitful than one of passive listening; and I developed this view mainly with regard to *social* education. Now I want to take up the same broad issues with regard to *intellectual* development. I would remind my readers again, however, that it is only for convenience that I look at these two aspects of the children's life in any degree of separation.

Now if I were writing a textbook of educational psychology, I should be expected to enter on a series of chapters on such topics as "the learning process", "habit", "memory", "imagination", "reasoning", and the like. And I should give the results of the very interesting experimental studies which have been made of these various mental processes in the minds of children; and then try to extract from them wise sermons for the classroom.

But (I am glad to say) I am not writing such a textbook. If my readers want a systematic study of these subjects, there are plenty about. I am myself much more interested in *the children* and the way in which they look at life, than in memory and imagination and reasoning and the apparatus of the textbooks. And I have no doubt that my readers, as practical teachers, share this prejudice with me: since it is *the children* with whom they have to deal.

Let us therefore look at the problem of intellectual development in the years from seven to eleven, as a whole, as *the child's* problem. For him, it is a question of *growth in understanding* the world around him, a world of things and of people. To that problem of understanding he will bring each and all of his abilities, in the measure of their development. The facts he is able to understand at eleven years of age may not be open to his grasp at seven. The ways in which he seeks to understand at seven may no longer seem significant to him at eleven. But at all ages we can be sure that he will be seeking some mode and some degree of understanding of the world around him, since he has to live in it, and to live safely.

It is easy, in the schools, to forget or overlook the strength of the child's spontaneous impulses towards understanding. The weight of the traditional curriculum and traditional teaching lies so heavily upon us and upon the children that their spontaneous interests have little chance to show themselves, and we, little leisure to notice them. But look at the same children out of school, in the buses and trams, at the Zoo, on Hampstead Heath, in the fields and woods of the country-side, or in the traffic-crowded streets. Watch their interest then in motors and railways and the pneumatic road-drill, in the farm and animal life. Listen to their questions. And, especially, listen and watch in the Infants' School years, before the children have become quite sophisticated. Take them before they have been taught to separate learning from playing and knowledge from life. Then you will not be able to doubt the strength and spontaneity of the wish to know and understand, within the limits of the child's intelligence.

In those earlier years, the spontaneous activities of children fall into three main groups: (*a*) the love of movement and of perfecting bodily skills; (*b*) the delight in make-believe and the expression of the world within; and (*c*) the interest in actual things and events, the discovery of the world without. And this last is as deeply rooted in the springs of the child's nature as the first two. Even the young child needs to know what is happening in the world around him. He can only find comfort and security in so far as he understands the behaviour of other people, on the one hand, and the probable responses to his own behaviour of fire and water and moving vehicles, on the other. It is not only that the burnt child dreads the fire. He wants to watch it and learn all about it—provided he has not been too badly burnt before he has had a chance to understand it. The thirst for understanding goes beyond the mere practical safeguarding of bodily survival. It springs from the child's deepest emotional needs, and with the intelligent child is a veritable passion. He must know and master the world to make it *feel* safe.

Now this can be seen to be plainly true of children at three and four years of age, and at six and seven. It is still true in the later years of childhood, although we sometimes miss its truth. We miss it, both because we are not looking for it, and because the child has often learnt to hide it. If he finds that we are not interested in his interests, but only in the things we think he ought to be interested in—well, children are on the whole docile and pliable, and will usually do their best to follow the lines we lay down. If in this effort the elasticity of their minds is over-stretched and lost, that is our fault rather than theirs.

One of the most striking illustrations I have met of how it is possible for the school to miss altogether the living interests of its children was given me by a remark I overheard one day. This was from a girl of ten and a half who was staying with me for a year, owing to illness in her own home. She was a highly intelligent child, full of eager inquiry about the world in general, and about birds and wild life in particular. We had walks together over the Cambridge fens, and journeys down the river. I was with her when she saw her first kingfisher, and knew the keen delight she felt. In living animals, in their skeletons and physiology, and in human anatomical diagrams alike, her concern was lively and sustained, and her knowledge growing without effort. I was therefore no little astonished when I heard her say, whilst telling other children about all the things she did in her own school at home (where she had an excellent academic record), "And we do 'Nature Study', but I *hate* it, it's always so dull!"

And dull indeed "Nature" or any other "Study" can be, unless it is kept vitally linked with the actual interests of the children in their everyday experience.

Let me take one more negative example. It may perhaps seem a little ungracious to illustrate what should

not be done, in these days when there are so many
happy instances of what can and should be done in the
schools. But sometimes the negative illustration brings
out most clearly what one wants to say. And this
instance is, I fear, of a kind still only too common.

I was carrying out some tests in a school in the
centre of a large town not far from London, a few
months ago, and was asked if I would make a study
of the children in the lowest group of the Girls' School.
These children were described to me as "extremely
backward" and "the despair of the teacher". And very
backward they turned out to be. When, after hearing
about them, and how difficult their teacher had found
it to awaken their minds at all, I went into their classroom, I was naturally eager to see what methods were
being used to stir them to effort and interest. And what
I saw was these thirty dull children, eight to nine years
of age, in a town school, sitting still and quiet each in
her own desk, each with one mangled primrose on the
desk in front of her, whilst a formal lesson on "pin-
eye" and "thrum-eye" was being given by the teacher!
I confess the mere thought of it made me feel dull and
backward myself! What possible meaning could this
have for those dim minds? If they had wandered in the
lanes and gathered the flowers themselves, from season
to season, it might have meant something, although
even that is doubtful with those particular children.

To appreciate the significance of "pin-eye" and
"thrum-eye", it is not enough to have an actual flower
to look at. One needs some understanding of the
pageantry of the seasons, the ability to bring together
in one's mind spring and autumn, this year and next.

One needs a lively curiosity into the how and why of what one sees in the lanes and woods. And one needs the full context of experience in the garden or the country-side before the question can have any meaning at all.

All this would have to be built up in the minds of town children, from the basis of their own experience, before "pin-eye" and "thrum-eye" could be more than the teacher's sound and fury. And with *backward* town children! What these dull minds needed was *doing*. If Nature Study, then sowing peas and beans and mustard seeds, each child caring for her own pot of living green, and sometimes making a sandwich for her lunch from the mustard and cress she had grown. Or, if primroses it had to be, then drawing and painting (however crudely) a great bunch or vase of them, or a picture of the flower woman selling them out of her basket in the streets. To have these things in the children's lives as a matter of course from day to day, to let them talk freely about them and act freely with them, linking them up with out-of-school life, would help to awaken both their delight in beauty and their interest in the life of plants. But to give formal lessons on isolated details, hard to observe and devoid of meaning for the children, must be barren in "Nature Study" and everywhere else.

Whether their lives are set in town or country, their intelligences dull or bright, the actual interests and the everyday experiences of our children offer us the only direct way into their hearts and minds. Even the dullest child has the need to understand his world in his own measure. And even the cleverest needs to have his life in the home and the street illumined and made more intelligible by what he learns in the school.

I want, then, to go on to a broad study of the spontaneous interests of children as they grow from seven to eleven, and to the characteristic ways in which they handle their experience at these different ages.

2. The Child *v.* the Curriculum

I spoke just now of the child's need to understand the world he lives in, and suggested that this need offers us the most fruitful approach to the work of the Primary School.

One of the first fruits of such an approach is our appreciation of the *unity* of the child's interests. For him, especially in the earlier years of the Primary School, the field of knowledge does not divide itself spontaneously into separate departments—"history", "geography", "nature study", "arithmetic", "English", and all the anatomy of the ordinary curriculum. *We* may parcel out his school day for him into these pigeon-holes, but the division hardly corresponds to anything in the child's own impulses. He is concerned with *things* and with *activities*—things to understand and things to do—rather than with "subjects".

Even the classification of his activities which I offered above is little more than a convenience for us, in talking about him. It is not a distinction felt deeply by the child himself. I suggested that when we watch the younger child's spontaneous activities, we can group the things he does into three main types: the love of bodily skill; the delight in make-believe; and the discovery of the external world. But in his actual behaviour, these three are closely intertwined. He passes readily from one sort of activity to another, and uses all of them to suit his purpose of the moment.

Take, as an example, the interest of the boy of five in railway engines. In a favourable setting, this will show itself freely in a variety of ways. Now he will be phantasying himself as an engine, "being" an engine, running round the room moving his arms as "cranks", and puffing and hissing as he has heard engines do. Then soon he may be modelling an engine in clay or drawing it in chalk. Presently he may be looking at a picture-book of engines, and asking endless questions about their respective sizes and destinations. And later he will be clamouring to be taken to the station to see real engines shunting.

These various ways of activity change together as the child develops. The skill of his hands, as it grows, serves more and more adequately both to reach his practical aims in the real world, and to express his feelings and phantasies. As his actual knowledge of the world broadens and deepens, his feelings and his sense of values change too. And pure make-believe passes gradually over into the pleasure of hearing the "true" story, and the imaginative effort of understanding real events in the present and the past.

The intelligent boy of ten or eleven is still eagerly interested in engines of all sorts. He will not now "be" an engine—he would scorn such childish phantasy. His imagination is now more deeply disciplined by real knowledge, and more fully at the service of his understanding. He admires the men who invent and improve engines and cars and aeroplanes, or those who use them to cross Africa or the Atlantic. In his dreams he becomes these brave adventurers, and he loves to hear of their perils and triumphs. He becomes interested in the history of the railway engine and the aeroplane, and in the way the latest model improves upon the latest but one. He goes (if he can) to museums to look at working models, and to gaze at the actual machines which made memorable flights. He has opinions about the respective merits of the different makes of cars and lorries and buses. He knows their prices, and often gathers, from here, there, and everywhere, an amazing amount of information about the details of their construction. And often he can identify the different makes by the particular sound of their engines heard at a distance. (I have known even a girl of ten say with certainty, "That's a Douglas", on hearing a motor-cycle chug a furlong away!) If he has the chance, the boy of eleven will ask questions and talk and argue and read about all these different aspects of his interest in engines—and write about them too. He often keeps notebooks full of drawings and tabulated facts.

I have taken this particular interest as one illustration of how the child's mind will (if it has the chance) range over the whole field of information pertinent to that interest, breaking down all the barriers which we set up between the relevant sorts of fact—history, geography, mechanics, economics; and will bring to the service of that interest every sort of activity—imagination, understanding, language, practical and artistic skill, alike. And yet, throughout, it will be an intensely concrete and practical interest—

an interest in _engines_ and the people concerned with them, not in the abstract sciences and systematised bodies of knowledge which engines illustrate.

I have described here the typical behaviour of the more intelligent children, and those who have the opportunity to follow out their developing interests. Children of poorer minds and poorer chances will not range so widely and deeply. Their interests will be simpler and cruder. Yet the movement of their minds remains essentially the same.

And I have looked at one of the out-of-school interests of the child, because it is in that direction that it is easiest for the teacher to see the child with a fresh eye, uninhibited by his habit-fixed notions of what the child should be and do. But the really skilled teacher does in fact base his teaching upon an implicit understanding of these ways of the child's mind, whatever "subject" is being presented. The inspired teacher of history knows how to harness the child's imaginings, his love of pictures and heroic tales, his delight in making and miming, to his genuine curiosity about people and events, for the slow building up of a knowledge of the objective past. The successful teacher of English knows how to draw upon all the child's wishes to communicate his real experiences and his feelings and imaginings alike. The good teacher of crafts knows not only how to subordinate his own pleasure in sheer skill and fine finish to his pupils' need for immediate achievement, but has, too, some appreciation of how this wish of the child to make things is but a part of his larger need to understand the world he lives in. If the craft teacher knows, as he should, the place of his craft in social and economic history, or the history of art, he will not wish to keep his own hours with the children isolated from the rest of their pursuits.

This intuitive sense of the child's problem as being the need to understand his life as a whole, has always inspired the great educational reformers. And it has often enabled the gifted practical teacher in the ordinary schools to transcend the barriers of the anatomised curriculum and time-table. Now, however, it is open to us all to share this inspiration. It is no longer an intuition of rare souls, but has become an everyday part of the everyday science of child psychology, based upon solid observations free to all. And soon it will be seen transforming every teacher's conception of the work of the school, and all the details of his practice.

It is when this sense of the vital function of the school, as a place where the child learns how to live, is lost or blurred, that handwork teaching (as an example) wavers between the Scylla and Charybdis of the formal syllabus on the one hand, and of the complete subordination of handwork to history and geography, on the other. If then either becomes a cut-and-dried programme of logically graded lessons, unrelated to the child's wishes or to his other pursuits—or is degraded to a mere rough and ready means of illustrating "the life of primitive man" or "children of other lands", etc., etc. Yet it need not be, and should not be, either of these. The child's wish to make and do is an integral part of his living, and for him a final good. His pleasure in skill stands on its own feet educationally—and yet it can also serve to forward understanding and make knowledge more precise. He will delight in making things that have stirred his imagination in a tale that has been told, no less than things he can use in work or play—a Crusader's sword, a model of a Norman castle, a model of an aeroplane or a boat, a railway signal that works, a rabbit hutch, a box for his pencils, a design for the cover of his notebook. The teacher's skill surely lies in drawing upon and satisfying all these motives towards the gradual mastery of the crafts for their own sake, as one part of the whole art of living.

When once this underlying unity of the child's interests is grasped, the time-table and the labelled curriculum both become good servants instead of the bad masters they have so often been. The time-table is no more than a mechanical aid to the proper quartering of the whole field of the child's problems. It is neither a natural nor a moral law, as people sometimes appear to think. It has more educational reason with the older groups of the Primary School than with the younger. Similarly with the division of interests and activities into the formal "subjects". This too is more justified with the older than with the younger groups, since with children of ten and eleven the different aspects of the pursuit of knowledge are *beginning* to be intelligible as distinct aims and ends. But even then the "subjects" have life and meaning only in so far as they are kept in close vital touch with the everyday concrete experience of the children and with each other.

3. The Development of Interests

Let us now look in more detail at the varying directions

of the child's wish to understand people and things in the world around him, as the years pass from seven to eleven. His *particular* interests change and develop, as he grows and adds to his skill and knowledge. His need to live fully is always there, but the content of a full life is not the same at every age. And "the world" as it comes to his mind as a young child differs in many ways from the world as it appears when he is a boy of eleven or a youth of eighteen. His impulses and his ripening experience act selectively upon facts and values, leading him to seek now this sort of knowledge or activity, now that. And the more closely our teaching is based upon an understanding of his particular needs at any age, the more nourishment will his mind be able to draw from it.

Where and how can we discover what the child's most active interests are at any age? I think we should look in two main directions. First, at all his freely chosen out-of-school pursuits, in the home, the garden, the playground, or the street—the games he plays, the things he makes with his hands, the books he reads, the questions he asks, the paths he wanders. And secondly, at all those school pursuits which he does with zest and pleasure. Whatever activity brings light to the eye and eagerness to the voice and gestures can be taken as a clue to some inner need of growth.

In both these settings we find we have to give pride of place, among the spontaneous interests of children in the Primary School years, to games and sports in the narrower sense. These are the chief means to physical and social growth. But I do not need to dwell upon them here, partly because I have already shown their great value in social education, partly because they do receive large recognition and understanding among us. Not yet enough *practical* recognition, it is true. There are still only too many children who suffer from lack of space and encouragement for the games of prowess and skill which are their great need.

Another group of activities which finds a deep response in the child of this period is singing, dancing, and miming. All these he will do spontaneously, and will follow with zest when helped to fuller art by skilled teaching. Such interests show no lessening in value and enjoyment when he passes from the Infants' to the Primary School. They should suffer none in opportunity and encouragement. A far larger place should be found for them in the new Primary Schools than was ever given them in the old.

It is sometimes thought that girls take more readily to acting in these years than boys, and it is true that the straightforward pleasure in "dressing-up" and the love of posing and personal display before an audience seems to be stronger and more naïve in the girls. Boys are more easily self-conscious and more readily aware of their own deficiencies. And they are earlier sensitive about personal dignity. But my own impression is that everything depends upon suiting the play and the part to the age and temperament of the boy actor. After all, what is he doing in his games of hunting and fighting and exploring, and even his Boy Scoutship, but play-acting? Only he does these for the sake of the doing, for the pleasure of losing himself in the new identity, rather than for the admiration of others. There is probably a genuine sex difference here. It is more natural and normal for the girl to offer herself for personal admiration than it is for the boy. The boy can only act successfully when his imagination is deeply stirred by the play itself, and he forgets the audience in the part. But then he will often put more creative intelligence and a fuller vigour into the acting than the girl. It is unwise and even rather cruel to force a part upon any boy that he feels to be "babyish" or "silly" or beneath his dignity. He should not be asked to be a fairy when he wants to be a bold buccaneer!

As I write, I hear again in my fancy the voices of two boy friends, brothers aged nine and seven, as I heard them a week or two ago. Their father had been reading *St. Joan* to them, and immediately they had wanted to act some of it themselves. They learnt most of the opening scene, between Robert de Baudricourt and his steward (it is hardly necessary to say that the elder actor cast the part of Robert for himself!), and acted it with the most entertaining colour and gusto. And the whole thing was quite spontaneous and untutored. (But, it may be noted, the great passion of both these boys at the moment is cricket!)

This pleasure of the Primary School child in miming links up directly with his earlier and cruder imitative play, when he became in turn a father, a doctor, a bus conductor, a soldier. But, as I have suggested, play-acting in the narrower sense is not the only inheritor of the earlier impulse to make-believe. The older boy's games of hunting big game, fighting the Germans, exploring the pathless wild, tracking down Indians, camping in the Antarctic, all those other thrilling adventures he loses himself in for hours at a time, are but the same make-believe impulses, now infused with a far greater real knowledge, and with a far more disciplined sense of what is possible and what merely phantastic. This sort of activity occupies a major part of the boy's free life all through these years, whenever and wherever it has the chance to be enjoyed, changing progressively in the direction of real achievement as knowledge and skill are added to.

And a great deal of real knowledge can be woven into the pattern of this play, as the genius of the Boy Scout movement saw. Map-making and map-reading, the understanding of weather signs, bird and animal lore, the ecology of the common flowering plants and trees in the country, architecture in the town, all the topography and geography of the district, whether town or country, have their beginnings here. The boy's growing independence of temper as he nears eleven and twelve, and his search for experience and real mastery of his environment, lead to his wandering farther and farther afield, whether in the city or the country-side. This is but his opportunity for wider and more systematic knowledge. It rests with us whether his migrant impulse is used to good account, or neglected until it turns to mere truancy and mischief.

I have spoken here of "the boy", but much of what I have said is nearly as true of girls as of boys, nowadays. Girls who have the chance are just as good at finding their way about the streets of a town or the paths on a wooded hill, and at reading the contour lines of a map. The more usual ease and sureness of older boys and men in these directions would seem to be almost if not entirely a matter of early experience and encouragement.

These joys of wandering in fields and woods, or even in markets and squares, are rich in contemplative moments, too—moments that may, even with so young children, find expression in verse or prose, if only we give room for free expression. I have just been reading a collection of delightful poems by children between seven and ten years, children of little more than an ordinary range of intelligence, who live at a country school where they have full freedom to write or speak as they feel. All the poems were interesting, and some were genuine literature. They were unmistakably the fruit, not only of a pleasure in words and poetic form, but of a direct sense of life that can only come from living it fully.

And what, now, of the joy of making things? This is hardly less a characteristic impulse of the Primary School years than those others I have spoken of. Professor Burt's inquiries led him to conclude that "making things" is one of the commonest forms of recreation at every age from nine to twelve. The boy will nearly always have something taking shape under his hands; and if he can choose freely, he will be making something to use in his play, whether for real or for dramatic ends. As he grows from seven to eleven, he moves on from the more tractable materials like plasticine, clay, and paper, to those needing more exact care, like wood and cardboard. And he will (even before seven, indeed) be most ingenious in adapting different sorts of materials to his immediate purpose, and using them in combinations that defy all syllabuses! (I remember my admiration for the way in which the children of five and six in my own school speedily discovered for themselves the adhesive value of plasticine, and began to make "aeroplanes" and "engines" out of wooden bricks stuck together most cleverly with plasticine.)

The years of growth bring increasing pleasure in the appropriateness of material, in correctness of detail, and in measurement and fit. Both boy and girl begin to take some pride in the quality of the work they do, as well as in the mere doing. But the time has not yet come, even in the later years of this period, for making exact measurement and fine finish the chief end of the work. That has in the past been one of the mirages of our teaching. We have often sacrificed design to neatness, invention to arithmetic, the child's free creative joy to theoretical grading of steps. But when we set accuracy and finish as our main goal, we give up the substance for the shadow, since these have yet no vital meaning for the children, and if pressed, only stifle his interest and effort. They will come in their time as hand and eye develop, and as the need to make and do is fully met.

We have long had some sense of the value to the child of making *real* things, but we still too often insist on choosing what he shall make; and we very often choose the wrong things. We too often prepare a syllabus of humdrum objects (trays and soap-boxes and paper-racks), interesting to the boy's elders, but striking no spark in him! As, again, Professor Burt has wisely suggested, things that move or aid movement—railway signals, scooters, sugar-boxes on perambulator wheels —are what stir the soul of the ordinary boy between seven and eleven. He will put great zeal into the making (or repairing) of things that he can use in his play, or things that help forward his other school interests. Both wood and cardboard, and the use of all the simpler tools, are easily within his range, if only *we* do not demand too high a level of finish and accuracy, but are willing to be as content as he is himself with something that suits his practical purposes.

Girls, too, nowadays, will often enjoy this sort of making. I have known several girls of seven to eleven who handled hammer and screwdriver and saw as well as any boy of the same age and experience, and could mend a wheelbarrow or a rabbit hutch quite satisfactorily. But, characteristically, the girl's interest in construction follows the line of such ancient domestic arts as sewing and weaving, basketry and pottery. These link on with the younger child's play with dolls and dolls' houses—which even in their own right may last on well into the Primary School ages. Most girls of nine to eleven will take pleasure in dressing dolls in the peasant costumes of different countries, or in historical costumes seen on a visit to a museum, or copied from authentic illustrations. They delight, too, in making whole families of those flat paper models of women and girls and babies, drawn and coloured and cut out, and various garments to dress the figures having little flaps to fold on to the cut-out model. Some girls will put hours of painstaking work into producing these—and here they seem to prefer copying or designing dresses and hats of to-day's fashions.

In general, girls of these years seem to take rather more pleasure in decorative drawing and designing in colour than boys do, the boys' interests running more to constructional design. Both boys and girls delight in free drawing and painting. Given the chance and the materials, they will spend much time on this activity, especially in indoor seasons. Their favourite subjects by far are human beings and moving things. They have no interest in copying other people's drawings, and none in representing the details of still-life objects with photographic accuracy. These things stir no vital response, nor are they of the least value as æsthetic education. By the movement of their own minds, children are never mere copyists. They are always creators. Chalk and brush are to them ways of expressing the *dramatic* values of the world, seen and felt through their own eyes. Their free drawings of men and animals, ships and motors *in action*, are often splendidly daring and powerful. They translate events into bold line and mass and colour, caring more for movement than for detail. Not seldom these drawings can challenge comparison with the great drawings of the Palæolithic caves, and they are far more akin to the work of modern artists than those who would aim at "teaching" the children in the schools sometimes know or care. Perhaps here more than anywhere, we need to *learn* from the children before we can have anything that is worth *teaching* them.

The Primary School child is not only a craftsman and an artist, however. He is also a property owner and a collector. These are the years when pockets are stuffed with heterogeneous odds and ends, despised by mothers, infinitely treasured by the owners. Bus tickets and tab cards at six or seven, stamps and shells, moths and butterflies at ten or eleven, show how the passion for ownership flings its net wider and wider as knowledge grows. The sense of property is strong and native in every boy and girl, and is never stronger than in this period of life. Starved and neglected, it runs underground and issues in envy and theft. Intelligently used, it offers one of the most valuable instruments of self-respect and of understanding. The child's pride in his own desk, his own books, his own tools, is a powerful educational lever. And his joy in collecting has endless possibilities for his school life. The class museum can be used to further most other interests—provided only it be brought together by the children themselves. A crude and fragmentary collection the children really have made themselves, even if it be just a collection of picture post-cards of London streets and buildings, or of birds' feathers picked up in the country lanes, will be more enlivening and more attended to than any elaborate and ordered collection of "specimens" inherited ready-made.

Those general interests we have already described can be found amongst all Primary School children other than the mentally deficient. Even the dull and backward love to wander and to play games, to make and mime, to draw and sing, however crude and unimaginative their achievements may be. But we can see another general interest absorbing more and more of the attention of intelligent boys and girls, although from the nature of the case it cannot stir the minds of the duller children. The lure of books now casts a growing spell over most boys and girls of these years, in homes where books are valued or tolerated. But the kind of reading sought changes as the children pass from seven to eleven, reflecting the general changes in their social and intellectual interests.

At the outset of the period, simple nature stories of the anthropomorphic type in which animals speak as human beings, and wind and weather are personified, are still enjoyed by both boys and girls. So is the more direct and realistic description of animal life, provided only it be told dramatically and vividly. But characteristically, this more detached type of animal story belongs to eight and nine years and later; and in these years children will hardly tolerate the crude talking-beast tale—unless it be as full of wit and wisdom as *Brer Rabbit*.

Fairy-tales of the terser description—Jack and the Beanstalk, Tom Thumb, Red Riding Hood—hold delights at six and seven. But it is at eight years of age that the classic fairy-tales of Grimm and Andersen and Andrew Lang have their greatest vogue. With some children, seven is the age of maximum pleasure in these tales; in others, nine years. But eight years appears to be the fairy-tale age of the great majority of children in many different parts of Europe and America.

Yet fairy-tales, loved and enjoyed as they are, do not represent the whole of the child's attitude to the world at this time. He has other moods in which stories of real events enthral him—tales of children in other lands and descriptions of the real life of animals. And here again we begin to get an interesting difference between boys and girls. Boys prefer to read of animals in the wild, and of heroic exploits in tracking, hunting, and taming them. Girls take the animals of the farm and the home more closely to their hearts.

At nine years, or even later, girls are still enjoying fairy-tales of the more mature type, whereas boys have definitely passed from under their spell. Boys become realists and lovers of matter-of-fact rather sooner than their sisters, and have begun to prefer stories of boy life and of real heroes.

It is at this age that the reading interest in general begins to take its strongest hold. Children under nine like short tales, soon accomplished. At nine and over, they begin to sustain their reading purposes longer, and will not fight shy of quite long books.

At ten years, fairy-tales fall off sharply in their appeal, even among girls. But myth and legend still hold their own. *Pandora's Box* and *The Miraculous Pitcher* are well loved. So are the quasi-historical legends such as *Robin Hood* and *William Tell* and the *Morte d'Arthur* cycle. A genuine interest in biography takes root here, and this, together with the growing delight in stories of travel and exploration, creates a new link with the historical and geographical studies of the school.

A certain number of the more intelligent boys begin now to read books on inventions and mechanics, and put some of the "Men Who Found Out"[1] into their gallery of heroes along with explorers and Elizabethan sailors and big-game hunters.

At eleven years, this new pleasure in books on electrical machines, aircraft, and engineering spreads to some extent even among ordinary children (if favourably introduced), and it gains an increasing hold on the systematic interest of the brighter boys. But tales of mystery and adventure are even more beloved, and

[1] A. Williams-Ellis, *Men Who Found Out*. G. Howe.

Henty, Jules Verne, Fenimore Cooper, and Sexton Blake come fully into their own. In this year of grace Edgar Wallace has also to be added to the list of the favourite authors of the eleven-year-old boy.

Neither of these boys' delights is common or compelling among girls. At eleven, they are reading the classic girls' stories such as *Little Women*, and tales of girls' schools and domestic life. *Black Beauty* is loved, and animal stories in general still hold their own. Many girls to-day, however, are beginning to read and to prefer their brothers' adventure stories, and this seems to indicate a definite and growing change in their education and outlook. But books on mechanics, engineering, and science appear to have almost no appeal to girls of eleven.

There is, however, another direction of reading interest which to-day it begins to be possible to add to our list, one which has so far remained largely undeveloped through lack of books; that is, the interest in the human body. The more intelligent boys and girls of eleven years are undoubtedly interested in the simpler facts of human anatomy and physiology, following on their earlier pleasure in natural history in general. There is still a great dearth of suitable books in this field, and much need for them. Here, waiting to be used and cherished, is an interest of the greatest possible educational value, one that can open up the whole field of personal and domestic hygiene and of general biology.

4. Children's Thinking

In the last section, I considered in broadest outline the chief interests of children between seven and eleven years, and the ways in which these interests change and develop through the period. But to complete even a cursory picture of children's minds in these years, one needs to look not only at the actual things they like to do and to learn about, but also at the ways in which their thought itself works. The modes of understanding open to the child change with growth and experience, as well as his actual interests.

People have, of course, long realised that children at different ages have somewhat different ways of seeing the world and thinking about it. But only in recent years have we begun to gather any detailed facts as to what those differences are. Until latterly we seemed to care more for making large generalisations about the few rough facts we had, than for adding to these data and making them more accurate.

We thought we were very wise indeed, for instance, when we talked about the development of the child "recapitulating" the biological development of the race, or paralleling the historical succession of "culture-epochs". And on the basis of such hazardous theories, we even tried to dictate what the child ought to be learning nowadays, at successive ages. Some, for example, have said that the teaching of history should begin with the caveman, solely on the ground of some supposed affinity between the minds of children of seven or eight and Palæolithic hunters.

Such premature theories of the nature of development, however, did little more than seduce us from the ampler study of the facts. We no longer find them particularly illuminating. And in recent years, we have begun to curb our appetite for generalisations, and to be willing to look more closely and patiently at the actual data.

I want to consider what broad facts have now been established, and then later to look at their practical bearings. But first it may be useful to indicate how important these practical applications may be, by a brief illustration.

There are still to be seen, alike in home and school, two quite different educational practices based upon opposing views as to whether or not young children "can reason". These two opposed views are sometimes acted upon even by the same educators, in different respects and on different occasions, since so few people work out clearly the theoretical basis of their behaviour to children. On the one hand, many people, assuming that children cannot reason until their early teens, when the "faculty" is supposed suddenly to appear, expect even intelligent children to obey all commands blindly and implicitly, and never attempt to give them any understanding of the grounds for rules and requests. And on this view all the routine activities are stressed— mechanical drill in the arts of reading and writing, rote memory in arithmetic, learning by heart in literature, "good habits" in social life. If the child does what he is told, gets habits of order and industry, fills his memory with crude facts, it is felt that he will be able to understand the why and the wherefore of all this when he comes to the years of reason, and be grateful to his educators for it.

On the other hand, even the same people often indulge in the practice of giving formal lessons on the abstract virtues—honesty, kindness, courtesy, tidiness, and the like. Even five-year-olds sometimes receive moral talks of this kind in school. And it is fondly imagined that such general descriptive terms can have real content to children in the Infants' and Primary School ages, and curb their impulses in actual situations. In this, young children are accredited with an ability to reason in abstract terms, and to control their behaviour by general ideas, which does in fact belong to much later years. All that such homilies succeed in doing is to bore the children, and to waste time that might have been used for some real experience of co-operating in games or handicrafts, or practical responsibility.

Neither of these extreme views (both still implicit in much of our ordinary educational practice) is well based. When do children begin to reason, then? And how? What is the relation between their reasoning, their language, and their practical activities? It is clearly of the greatest value for parents and teachers to know whether, when, and how reasoning develops, and all the ways of children's thought in earlier and later periods.

The first investigators to bring together any large body of reliable experimental data as to the ways of children's thinking at different ages were those who, like Binet and Burt, wanted for practical reasons to measure the growth of intelligence. In earlier sections I discussed the value of tests of intelligence for the purpose of distinguishing between the ability of different children of the same age, and for grading groups of children within the school. Now I want to look at what intelligence tests have revealed about the average child's ways of thought in successive years of development. I can then go on to Piaget's important studies in this field; and, finally, will say something about my own direct observations of thinking in young children.

The Binet scale is not the best instrument for comparing children's thought at different ages, since the questions it offers to the child are very mixed, and many of them are scarcely problems of thought. Yet it does reveal many significant facts for this purpose; and if one picks out of the series of questions those which do call for actual thinking, and compares the sort of thing children can do in different years, one gets some sense of the direction which development takes.

Look first at the series of "problems of comprehension". At four years, the average child can deal successfully with such questions as "What must you do when you are sleepy? cold? hungry?" At six years, with such as "What ought you to do if it is raining when you start to school?" ". . . if you find that your house is on fire?" ". . . if you are going somewhere and you miss your bus?" At eight, with "What ought you to do if you broke something that belonged to someone else?" ". . . if you find that you're likely to be late when you're on your way to school?" ". . . if another boy hit you by accident without meaning to?" And at ten, with the following: "What ought you to say if someone asks you what you think of a boy you don't know very well?" "Why should we judge a person more by what he does than by what he says?" And "What ought you to do before beginning something very important?"

Now how do the later of these problems differ from the earlier? What is it that the ten-year-old can do and the four-year-old cannot?

In the first place, he can deal with issues that are less concrete and more general. Being sleepy or hungry is a direct sensory experience, simple yet vivid and intensely real. The mere mention of it will call up clear images of the feeling itself and of what happens when one has that feeling. "Beginning something important" involves much more general ideas—it is not a particular experience, but a class of experiences. The child is pretty sure, when he is asked the question, to think of this or that actual experience of such a kind, but the images aroused are not likely to be so full and of such a direct bodily flavour as with the earlier questions.

The situation to be dealt with is not only less concrete and more general—it is also much more complex. To answer any of the ten-year questions, the child has to bring together in one act of comparison and judgment a great many varied experiences with other children and with grown-ups, people saying and doing this or that on this or that occasion—and to get the heart out of all these in one complex judgment. And such a problem is less immediately personal, too, than the question of what to do when one is hungry, or when one's house is on fire. But even with these two latter questions, one can see how much advance is made between four and six years of age. Every child has been actually cold and hungry and sleepy. Not every child of six has had his own house on fire, or even seen any house on fire. But he is by now able to make use of other people's experiences, communicated in words and pictures, and linking up with what he has actually seen of fires in general, to understand very clearly what he should do *if* his house were to be on fire.

One significant difference in the problems which older and younger children can tackle is thus the actual range of direct and indirect experience drawn upon. And the "ifness" itself (which one sees still more clearly with eight-year questions) is obviously of the utmost importance in the development of thought. Here we see something of the early growth of the ability to hold a mere possibility in thought, and forecast its consequences without having necessarily experienced them beforehand. I shall suggest later on that we can see the first beginnings of the ability to entertain hypotheses, "If such and such a thing happens, then so and so will follow," or "Then I shall do so and so," in the imaginative play of quite little children.

Meanwhile, even on the limited material so far considered we can see that development goes on, not by the sudden appearance from time to time of entirely new abilities. It shows itself rather in a progressive increase in the child's power to handle issues that are relatively remote from immediate experience, less concrete and more general in character, more complex in type, needing a wider background of knowledge, and involving a greater element of "ifness", or hypothesis, than those he can deal with in the earlier years.

One way of summing up all these lines of change, in

harmony with recent technical researches in psychology, is to say that the child shows a growing ability to appreciate more and more complex *relations*, and to handle these relations more and more clearly and precisely. If one takes another of the tests given at successive ages in the Binet series, one can illustrate the same point. A picture shown to the child of four, with the request, "Tell me all about it," leads the average child of this year to give the names of several of the things he can see in the picture, pointing to this and that in turn. These isolated items are not brought together into one descriptive whole; they are just enumerated in a staccato fashion: "chair—table—lady—little girl" and so on. We can of course hardly doubt that some of the simpler relations between these various objects are in fact apprehended to a greater or lesser extent. The child probably sees that the lady is sitting on the chair, the loaf is on the table, the cat on the floor, the child crying, and so on. He has not yet, however, the power to separate out these relational elements, attend to them as such, and express them in appropriate sentences. His naming probably means all this, in an inarticulate way. But the child of seven can articulate these relational elements and put them into words. "The baby's crying, and the mummy is looking at her." "There's a little Dutch girl, and she's crying, and her mummy is sitting down." And the child of twelve in his turn can do much more than this. He does not now stop at the mere description of what is actually seen, but goes on to still larger wholes of thought, involving relations of cause and of motive. "The baby is crying because she is hungry and the mother hasn't anything for her to eat."

"The little girl's been naughty, and her mother is cross."

That is to say, the child can now bring to bear upon the sight of the picture, not only memories of similar situations which she has seen or heard of or actually experienced, but also previous reflections upon why and when children cry, and how their behaviour is related to that of the grown-ups round them. The pictured behaviour of mother and child forms a unity which is not only appreciated as a single whole, but which can also be analysed in thought into its constituent facts and the relations of cause and effect between them; and these more complex relations can be set out in words.

The development of thinking in the child thus largely rests upon: (*a*) the growth of his ability to hold together in one act of understanding a larger number of facts and relations; and (bound up with this) (*b*) the ability to pass from the simpler relations between things to the more subtle and complex. Both these points are shown very interestingly in another of the Binet tests, that of the comparison of weights. At five years of age, the average child can tell us correctly which is the heavier of two boxes or blocks of the same size and appearance but different weights. Not until four years later can he correctly grade a series of five similar weights. This latter task is very much more complex, because he cannot compare all five together directly by actual sensation. He can only compare two at once, then two others, and then has to compare the *memory* of the first judgment with the present actual one—and so on. The whole series has to be kept in mind as a whole, and each of the separate sensory judgments related to this whole. The problem thus calls for a great increase in the ability to hold relations together in thought, and to build them into larger wholes.

These general directions of development can be seen most clearly and significantly, however, when we take, not a heterogeneous series of tests such as the Binet scale, but a more homogeneous series of problems such as Burt's graded reasoning scale. This scale is probably known to all those of my readers who have interested themselves in tests at all, and I shall need to quote only three or four of its items to bring out their bearing on the present issue.

At six and a half, for instance, children can deal with this question: *Tom runs faster than Jim: Jack runs slower than Jim. Which is the slowest of the three?* At eight years: *I don't like sea voyages: and I don't like the seaside. I must spend Easter either in France, or among the Scottish hills, or on the South Coast. Which shall it be?* At ten years: *There are four roads here: I have come from the south and want to go to Melton. The road to the right leads somewhere else: straight ahead it leads only to a farm. In which direction is Melton—north, south, east, or west?* And at twelve years: *Field-mice devour the honey stored by the humble-bees: the honey which they store is the chief food of the humble-bees. Near towns, there are far more cats than in the open country. Cats kill all kinds of mice. Where, then, do you think there are most humble-bees—in the neighbourhood of towns or in the open country?*

One has only to read these selections from Professor Burt's series, remembering that they are part of a properly standardised scale, that is to say, they are problems which the majority of children of the given years actually *do* succeed in solving, to realise two very important general truths. First, that it is quite false to say, as it used to be said, that reasoning only begins in the teens. Children of less than the Primary School ages can and do reason very effectively in formal terms provided only that the premises to be dealt with are few, simple, fairly concrete, and familiar. As Burt himself stated it when first publishing the results of his research,[1] "All the elementary mental mechanisms essential to formal reasoning are present before the child leaves the Infants' department, i.e. by the mental age of seven, if not somewhat before." And, secondly, that: "Development consists primarily in an increase in the extent and variety of the subject-matter to which those mechanisms can be applied, and in an increase in the precision and elaboration with which those mechanisms can operate. The difficulty of a test depends upon its complexity." And, Burt goes on to say, "The precise nature of the connections—temporal, spatial, numerical, causal, etc., and of their interconnections— hypothetical, disjunctive, etc., are of relatively little importance." In other words, whenever we seem to have a sudden emergence of a new sort of ability at a particular age, such as the ability to reason about distances or times or causes, or to argue in "ifs" and "thens", the apparent suddenness of growth is due only to our not observing its earlier stages closely enough. If we make each *kind* of problem simple enough and clear enough, even children in the Infants' School years will be able to deal with it.

[1] C. Burt: "The Development of Reasoning in School Children." *Journal of Experimental Pedagogy*, Vol. V, pts. ii and iii.

I do not doubt that readers will begin to see something of the bearing of these facts upon methods of teaching in the lower groups of the Primary School years. It *is* most significant for teaching method that even the younger children are not to be looked upon as creatures of mere habit and memory, but as being able to reason and argue and draw conclusions, if we but make the appropriate opportunity for them.

And yet, of course, broad differences do remain between the older and the younger children, due to the cumulative effect of the slow growth from simple beginnings. It is, for instance, a striking fact that the ability to criticise other people's logic and resist fallacies, is later in ripening than straightforward constructive reasoning. To return to the Binet scale for a moment (as revised by Burt), it is not until ten years of age that the average child can deal with such "absurdities" as "I have three brothers, Jack, Tom, and myself"; or, "A man said: 'I know a road that is downhill all the way to the town, and downhill all the way home.'" Not until ten years can children both see that these statements are absurd, and explain satisfactorily the nature of the absurdity. Yet this does not mean, of course, that no absurdities of any kind or degree of difficulty can be appreciated by children before that age. So far as I know at present, no psychologist has yet attempted to construct a scale of "absurdities" suitable for younger children—Dr. Ballard's well-known series, for instance, starts from very much the level of the Binet examples, and moves upwards to greater degrees of difficulty. Yet I have little doubt that it could be done, for the spontaneous remarks of quite young children often show a sense of logical absurdity on simpler levels.

5. Children's Errors

Having now looked at some of the broad facts revealed by the work of Binet and Burt with regard to the reasoning ability of children at different ages, I want to turn to Piaget's studies in the same field. Piaget has been primarily interested in children's *errors* of thought. He has wanted to know what children *do* when they fail to reason, and what goes on in their minds when they do not succeed in giving the "right" answer to a question. In his own words, Piaget attempts "to describe the obstacles which the child has to overcome in order to attain scientific thought".[1] When, for instance, it was established that not until ten years of age can the average child satisfactorily explain what the absurdity is in such a statement as "I have three brothers, Jack, Tom, and myself," Piaget inquired into what they actually do when they are faced with such a problem, and fail to deal with it logically. *Why* can they not get the correct answer?

In the course of these and other studies, by very ingenious methods of experiment and questioning, Piaget has gathered a great wealth of the most interesting facts about the form and the content of children's thought about the world at all ages below eleven or twelve. Here I cannot do more than mention a few of his conclusions relevant to the main purpose of this short book.

[1] *British Journal of Educational Psychology*, Vol. I, pt. ii, p. 134.

Let us start from the "three brothers" test. When a child failed to see this absurdity, Piaget asked him to arrange the sentence "so that there should not be anything silly in it", and followed up the point by further questioning as to the child's ideas of family relationships in general. What he found was that children failed to deal with this problem mainly because they were not yet able to think in terms of reciprocal relations. They understood what it is to *have* a brother, but not what it is to *be* one. They did not seé that each member of the family is the brother (or sister) *of* each, and that each can say "*my* brother" of every other member. That is to say, they had no notion of *membership* of a whole with mutual relations between the parts. And they experienced a similar difficulty with regard to the mutuality of the relation between parent and child.

To make the point clear, I will quote one of Piaget's examples of a conversation, one that shows a child of eight years struggling to master these facts of relationship, when pressed by questioning. Gys is asked: "Have you a brother?" "*Yes.*" "And your brother, has he got a brother?" "*No.*" "Are you sure?" "*Yes.*" "And has your sister got a brother?" "*No.*" "You have a sister?" "*Yes.*" "And she has a brother." "*Yes.*" "How many?" "*No, she hasn't got any.*" "Is your brother also your sister's brother?" "*No.*" "And has your brother got a sister?" "*No.*" "How many brothers are there in your family?" "*One.*" "Then you are not a brother?" (He laughs) "*Yes.*" "Then your brother has got a brother?" "*Yes.*" "How many?" "*One.*" "Who is it?" "*Me.*"[1]

[1] J. Piaget, *Judgment and Reasoning in the Child*, p. 86.

Such an example shows clearly how hard it is for a child below a certain mental age to see the relations between his brother and himself *from the point of view of the brother*. And it is this absoluteness of the child's judgments, seen from himself as centre, which makes him also unable to deal adequately with problems involving *relative* positions in space. For example, in Burt's reasoning scale, the following problem can only be dealt with successfully at nine years: Three boys are sitting in a row; Harry is to the left of Willie; George is to the left of Harry. Which boy is in the middle? Piaget pursued this question with children of earlier years, and concluded that the child's difficulty lay in his failure to appreciate the mutual *relativity* of right and left positions in space.

These and many other detailed studies of children's logic led Piaget to certain general conclusions about the stages of development which children's thinking passes through, and the way in which their logic and their thought are affected by their social development at successive ages.

He distinguishes, first, a broad general stage of social and intellectual development which he calls "ego-centrism", a stage which lasts until round about seven to eight years. In this phase, children (on Piaget's views) are not only self-centred in their wishes and social behaviour. They are so in all their thinking, too. They have an implicit belief in their own ideas, and take it for granted that everyone believes exactly the same as they do. Their opinions about things in the world are not arrived at by discussion and argument with others. Indeed, Piaget thinks, they never do discuss or argue with each other in any real sense. They just do not realise that other people may see things differently, and that their own views may have to be modified by the opinions of others. When a group of such young children are together, they say things to each other, of course; but usually their remarks are not meant to evoke any response, let alone an argument. Their talk is a series of unrelated exclamations, rather than true conversation. And any questions they may ask have a rhetorical purpose rather than one of genuine inquiry. Like Pontius Pilate, they do not wait for an answer.

It is, on Piaget's view, this naïve unquestioning assumption of children that the world *is* as it *seems* to be from their own angle of judgment, that lies at the root of their failure in verbal logic. Until he has realised that there *are* contrary opinions and that things may seem differently from the standpoint of other people, the child has no spur to reflecting upon the *way* in which he thinks. And without such reflections upon the way in which he thinks, he cannot learn to think logically.

Thus Piaget found evidence to show that the younger children cannot handle the logical relations involved in the use of "because" and "therefore". They cannot keep clearly apart in their minds statements that exclude or contradict one another, but tend to jumble them all up together in a mere "togetherness", substituting the notion of "and" for that of "but" or "because". They commonly reverse the relation of cause and effect; and (like many adults) argue from one particular instance to another, making no appeal to general propositions.

Now at or about seven to eight years, the child's social instincts (Piaget thinks) begin to develop.

Through his growing wish to play *with* others, not just amongst others, he becomes more aware of the point of view of his playmates. He begins to realise that they may think differently about things from the way he does, and that truths in general, like positions in space, may be relative to the standpoint from which they are judged. And as he learns to adapt his *actions* to others, so also he gradually comes to *think* reciprocally, and to criticise his thinking from the point of view of a common logic.

His verbal thinking, however, lags far behind his practical logic. He can deal with the problems of right and left, of degree and order, and of social relations, *in practice*, long before he can handle the same issues in words, and in thought divorced from action. Throughout all the Primary School years he manages all these things with practical ease, but not until the end of the period (Piaget holds) does he begin to show any *verbal* facility in reasoning. He may begin to be interested in mechanical causes and effects at about eight or nine years of age, but he has little success in causal *thinking* until eleven or twelve years.

Now with most of these broad general conclusions about the child's ways of development in judgment and reasoning, those who have had experience with children will agree. It is quite clear that the practical appreciation of spatial and causal relations does come to the child before the ability to deal with them in thought alone. It is clear, too, that the young child does see the world largely from the point of view of his own immediate desires, judging things simply as related to himself; and that his contacts with other people must help to wean him from this self-centredness to understanding of reciprocal relations. It is obvious also that the child's developing social relations must act as a powerful stimulus to verbal expression and to clarity and consistency of thought. Piaget has shown us vividly and fully the way in which the various aspects of social and intellectual development are bound up together.

And yet his first statements of his general conclusions about mental development did not give us a finally satisfactory picture of ordinary boys and girls as we know them in everyday life. A good deal of qualification was needed—and has actually been made by Piaget in later discussion with his critics.[1] His own love of theoretical systems and clearly ordered "stages" led him at first to see the various phases of mental development as far more definite and sharply bounded than they really are. In actual children, the different "stages" of growth overlap and intermingle. A child may be able to think logically in one direction, and yet fall back on magic and phantasy in another, according to the mood of the moment, or the particular situation in which he finds himself.

As Burt showed us long ago, children even as young as seven and eight can and do reason, not only in practical modes but in *words* also, provided only that the problem is simple, concrete, and familiar enough. Every mother knows that tiny children are occasionally interested in the way things work long before the ages at which Piaget credits them with any concern for mechanical causality, although they cannot follow this

[1] *Vide*, e.g., *Mind*, Vol. XL, No. 159, pp. 137–160. *British Journal of Educational Psychology*, Vol. I, pt. ii, pp. 130–139.

out in any sustained way. And no one who has played with a group of young children free to talk can doubt that argument and exchange of opinion does sometimes occur at an early age, alongside the most naïve ego-centric dogmatism.

In general, the difference between one "stage" and another is always a matter of more or less. The younger children will fall into the errors of "ego-centrism" more readily and more often than the older—but even grown-ups do so from time to time.

6. The Beginnings of Reason

I want now to speak of some of my own researches into the development of thought for comparison with Piaget's evidence. These dealt mainly with children under eight years, but as they were unusually intelligent children (with an average mental ratio of 131), the facts throw a good deal of light upon the thinking of older children of more ordinary ability. I want to outline particularly those general conclusions which certainly hold good of Primary School pupils.

I must first, however, say something of the conditions under which these observations were made,[1] since these have a direct bearing upon the practical suggestions I shall offer later on.

The main characteristic of the environment in which these children spent their days was that it fostered the children's own doing and thinking. The physical setting and the educational technique alike were designed to call out *the children's* activity, rather than

[1] *Vide* my *Intellectual Growth in Young Children.* Routledge, 1930, Schocken Books, 1966.

the teacher's. The function of the teachers was to stand by, ready to make suggestions when these seemed appropriate, but mainly to follow out the spontaneous interests of the children, and to foster their inquiries, experiments, and discoveries, in whatever direction these might take. For example, the children's embryonic interests in causes and effects in the physical world were followed up when they arose. An instance or two might make this clear. "The children discovered by accident that a piece of modelling wax which had been dropped on the hot-water pipes had melted. They were very excited about this; and began to try other things on the pipes to see whether they would melt—plasticine, chalk, wood, and so on. Talking about this led to a discussion as to whether these things would melt better in the fire, and the children went on to try various things in the bonfire in the garden. This was one of the threads of interest which led us presently to give the children a Bunsen burner and the necessary accessories for trying out these experiments, as these made it so much easier for them to see the results clearly. Another thread was their interest in melting ice and snow, which began on a snowy morning the same winter, and which was at first carried on by putting jars on the hot-water pipes."

"Some of the children noticed the white china weights on the pulleys by which the electric lights could be lowered and raised. They asked what these were, and pulled them down to look at them. They were very interested in the mechanism, but the pulleys were far too high for the children to see them clearly. We therefore got a number of light aluminium pulleys which could be fixed on the walls of the schoolroom, or over the sandpit. The children came to understand these by using them in their play."

Their interest in making and miming, dancing and singing, and in make-believe, was, however, met and encouraged quite as adequately as their concern with pulleys and the action of water and fire. It was indeed an essential part of our technique that they should be free *either* to inquire into the real world or to express their own phantasies in make-believe, as they felt the need.

Another very important element in these children's life was their freedom to talk. They were always free to say what was in their heads, to ask questions, and to argue. This opportunity to express thoughts and feelings undoubtedly fostered both their verbal reasoning and their objective interest in the world.

As was to be expected, the encouragement to practical activities of all sorts developed their "practical judgments" to a higher degree of sense and skill than most children of the same ages show. And it led them to evince a very considerable interest in physical causality, arising out of their practical problems in play and in making things. This concern was shown in varying degrees by different children and at different times; but it appeared in all of them, and is probably a universal interest amongst intelligent children of these ages.

Furthermore, the children found themselves able to express in words their understanding of mechanical causality when occasion arose. (In the examples quoted, the ages of the children should be particularly noted.) When, for instance, one day some of the children slipped on the stairs in the schoolroom and made some remark about the steepness of these stairs, "Dan (5 ; 1) said, 'Yes, that's because there's not enough room at the bottom. If there was more room, we could push the bottom of the stairs out, and they wouldn't be so steep.'"

Or again: "Dan (5 ; 9) was sitting on his tricycle in the garden, backpedalling. A grown-up said to him, 'You're not going forward, are you?' 'No, of course not, when I'm turning them the wrong way.' She asked, 'How does it go forward when it does? What makes it?' He replied, in a tone of great scorn for her ignorance, 'Well, of course your feet push the pedals round, and the pedals make that thing go round (pointing to the hub of the cranks), and that makes the chain go round, and the chain makes that go round (pointing to the hub of the wheel), and the wheels go round, and there you are!'"

Another day: "Christopher and Priscilla wanted some paper bags to burst, and as there weren't any, decided to make some. Someone asked, 'How will you make them?' 'We'll sew them,' said Christopher. Frank (5 ; 11) said at once, 'That won't do. They won't burst, because the air will come out of the holes you make.'"

And Christopher (5 ; 2) told an adult one day, "When you explain a thing, you say it's like something else!"

These examples show, too, how much genuine interchange of opinion went on amongst the children. There was very considerable argument and discussion at all times—as when, for instance, the children were modelling engines and railway lines, and Frank (5 ; 3) insisted to the others that "the sleepers are always *underneath* the lines," correcting another child's model.

Or when "looking at the picture of a whaling ship with smaller boats hung over the sides, one of the children said, 'Those are lifeboats.' 'No,' said Paul (4 ; 0), 'lifeboats don't be on the side of the ship, they are on the cliff in a long shed.' "

I pointed out earlier that one difference between the reasoning abilities of older and younger children lay in the extent to which hypothesis or "ifness" plays a part. The intelligent boy of eleven or twelve can follow out the possible conclusions of given premises without having to try them out in action. The younger child is less able to do this. In his imaginative and constructive play, however, we can see the first beginnings of such hypothetical reasoning; as in the following instance: "A lady visitor came who talked to the children about her journey from Australia. When they heard that she was several weeks on the boat, Dan (4 ; 1) said, 'Then you'd have to have beds on the boat,' and one of the others, 'Did you have breakfast and supper on the boat?' 'Yes!' Dan: 'Then you'd have to have tables and chairs.' " Or in this: "The children wanted to re-paint the seesaw, and Joseph was eager to do it at once. It was pointed out to him that if they did do it to-day, they would not have the use of it for some days, until the paint was dry. Nevertheless, he wanted to begin at once. James (5 ; 2), however, said, 'It would be a good thing to wait until the last day of term, and then it would have all the holiday to dry in.' "

These examples of children's reasoning suggest how the higher levels of thought and reasoning develop out of the lower. Through the drive of his practical interests, the child is carried on from the simpler and more obvious aspects of experience to the more complex and subtle. His thought becomes gradually disciplined by actual knowledge of causal relations in the external world. We can see, too, how the same child, in one and the same year of his growth, can be taken up, now by pure phantasy and the magical fulfilment of wishes, and now by the facts of the external world. According to the mood and situation of the moment, he will pass from magic to science and back to magic again. The very children who gave such clear instances of dis-interested reasoning and understanding of causality nevertheless offered from time to time very striking examples of purely "ego-centric" phantasy and magical beliefs. An instance of this occurred one day when the kettle was on the stove boiling, and a jet of steam coming out of the spout. Dan (5 ; 9) and Priscilla (7 ; 7) waved their hands at it, and Dan spat at the kettle. When someone asked him, "Please don't spit," he replied, "But I wanted to stop that coming out!"

This admixture of common-sense and the appre-ciation of cause and effect in the real world, on the one hand, with "ego-centric" phantasy on the other, can, however, be found in all children, if we observe them not just under experimental conditions, but over the whole field of their behaviour. Ursula, for example, whom I quoted in illustration of the intelligent young child's logical criticism of grown-up inconsistency (p. 90) offers us (all within the same fifth year) the clearest examples of good sense alongside equally clear ex-amples of the "ego-centric" rejection of such reality as cuts across her wishes. For an instance of a piece of matter-of-fact good sense, take the following conversation. Her nurse had given her half a grapefruit for supper, and Ursula said that it had "a lot of juice". N. "I think it's because I've taken out the core and pips and it's easy to get the juice." U. "Perhaps it's the bottom half." N. "What do you mean?" U. "Well, if it were the bottom half it would be more juicy." N. "Why would it?" U. "Because at the bottom the juice would run to the bottom. I hope I shall always have that half." N. "Then who would have the top halves?" U. "Dora could have those, 'cos she's smaller."

Or take her generalisation in a moment of quiet reflection after questioning her mother about the different times when father, mother, and sister, etc., have their baths: "All men and ladies and girls and boys and little children and babies and nurses are different and do different things, don't they?"

Again, see the dawning consciousness of her own mental processes shown in the following remark to her mother: "Last summer Ann said to me 'Can you do this?' and I said 'Yes,' and she said 'Do it now,' and I said 'I don't *want* to now!' But I said that because I didn't really know *how* to do it—and I didn't want her to know!"

After these examples of Ursula's waxing sense of logic and of that awareness of herself which on Piaget's view is a necessary foundation for a sense of logic, listen to her "ego-centric" demands when one morning her usual day's programme had been upset by a change in circumstances. About the middle of the morning she burst out with violent howls: "I want the time back that has gone! I *must* have the morning begin again. You *must* make the morning begin again. You *must*! But you *must*!!! It's all Daddy's fault for coming in the room. I wanted to play with my paper dollies." (A game she likes to play in a room quite alone.) Mother: "Well, you've got all the rest of the morning." U., weeping violently, "No, it won't do. It's not long enough. You *must* make the morning begin again."

And finally, listen to the evidence of her inner conflict between "ego-centrism" and the demands of social reason. Ursula had been taken to see "Peter Pan" and enjoyed it intensely. The morning after, she begged to be taken again that very day, and when told this was not possible, she stormed and pleaded again and again. After many bitter tears, she then turned on her mother and said, "You shouldn't have *taken* me yet, Mummie, you shouldn't have taken me yet. You should have waited till I was older!" "But why?" asked her mother. "Because then I should have been more sensible!" Here we can hear the actual struggle between her intelligence and her imperious desires, as well as her awareness of herself from the point of view of older years.

These children thus not only offer us both magical and scientific ways of thought. They show us, too, the latter developing out of the former, under the pressure of facts, or of other people's opinions. When Tommy, for instance (4 ; 2), modelled a goose and told Miss B. "It's flying," moving it in the air, he was asked, "How can it fly when it hasn't any wings?" His first reply was, "The wings are inside"; but presently he modelled the wings on to it. He thus showed himself ready to accept corrections and able to make use of other people's criticisms of his first "ego-centric" impulses.

The same child illustrates, too, the broad general point I made in criticising Piaget's clear-cut "stages" of development. It is agreed that the young child is relatively unable to understand reciprocal relations. Yet we can often see the first beginnings of this understanding at quite early ages. As in the following instance: "The children had seen me opening the skylight and came to do it too, taking turns. One of them said, 'Me after Tommy,' and then Tommy (2 ; 11) himself said, 'Me after Tommy.' He at once drew my attention to this, laughing and repeating it—'I said "Me after Tommy." ' " Here one obviously has an awareness of the difference between the point of view of a person as seen by himself and as seen by others, an awareness which foreshadows the later sense of reciprocal relationship. And one sees, too, the first dawning of the sense of logical absurdity.

7. Some Practical Conclusions

To summarise all this evidence briefly, it is clear that the sayings and doings of children show how false is any view of mental development which sees it as an affair of fixed stages. Although abstract reasoning and verbal formulation belong characteristically to the years beyond the Primary School, yet this is clearly only a matter of relative emphasis, not by any means an absolute distinction. Even in the Infants', let alone the Primary School ages, children are by no means unreflecting creatures of rote and habit. Nor is the

Primary School child *merely* a person of "practical judgment", unable to argue or to reason in words.

The evidence quoted shows, too, that one of the main stimuli to the expression of reasoning in words comes to young children from their practical interests in play, and from the discussions and arguments which these play interests give rise to. When occasion calls for it, they break into theoretical statement, although they cannot yet *sustain* verbal thinking. And whilst the ability to think in hypothesis, so essential an element in scientific thinking, does not appear in any systematic way until eleven or twelve years, yet it can be seen springing up here and there in the talk of children very much earlier. It is called out by imaginative play, or by the child's need to forecast the future in his practical pursuits.

Now all these qualifications of more and less are of the utmost significance for education. It is most important that teachers should realise not only that children in the Primary School are *mainly* practical people, concerned more intimately with things than with principles, but also that the interest in principles is born from the interest in things. The more abstract reasoning of the adolescent boy and girl has its beginnings and first development in the practical pursuits of the earlier years. And if we are to foster the higher intellectual activities, we need to understand *how* they grow from the simpler.

This, however, is but one more illustration of the main theme of this book. Throughout, I have been attempting to give the practical teacher some sense of the value of understanding what goes on in the child's mind in the different years of the Primary School. I have had no space to go into the practical problems of the schoolroom in any systematic detail, but I have tried to offer enough actual instances from point to point to illuminate the general direction of my argument. I should like now to sum up the main considerations for the practical work of education in the Primary School which seem to me to emerge from the psychological facts considered. Certain broad practical principles can be seen, which, if fully understood, would profoundly affect the whole organisation of life in the Primary School, as well as all the details of the curriculum and of methods of teaching.

In the first place, it is clear that the practical bearings of the study of children's thought which we have just made fall into line with the conclusions suggested by our previous study of their interests at different ages, and of the course of their social development. From all these directions, one is brought back to the fundamental conclusion that throughout the Primary School years, no less than in the years under seven, it is *the children's activity* that is the key to their full development. Whether we are observing the great need of the child for active movement as a condition of physical growth and of poise and skill, the ways in which he is led out of the narrow circle of his own egoistic desires and naïve assumptions about the world, or the situations which provoke verbal reasoning and argument, we come back at every point to the view that it is the child's doing, the child's active social experience and his own thinking and talking that are the chief means of his education. Our part as teachers is to call out the children's activity, and to meet it when it arises spontaneously. We can give them the means of solving problems in which they are actively concerned, but we cannot fruitfully foist problems upon them that do not arise from the development of their own interests. And their native interests in things and people around them —the street, the market, the garden, the railway, the world of plants and animals—do in fact offer us all the opportunities we need for their education.

In the second place, the children's activity in these years, whether in history or geography, mathematics or nature study, is most fruitful when it is most concrete and practical, having to do with real things that can be seen and handled and made and measured. This is especially true in the earlier years of the Primary School, but even at ten and eleven it is still one of the most significant facts about children. Words cannot yet be substituted for things, although they can be used to formulate the experience of things. Theoretical reasoning is a dead letter to the child unless it is closely anchored to practical issues.

And yet, none the less, these children need the *opportunity* of verbal reasoning. They should not be expected to talk or listen *instead* of doing, but they should be allowed to talk about *what* they are doing. And whilst *our* talking to them (or at them) may be barren, our readiness to talk *with* them is quite a different thing. Our third general conclusion is thus that another great need of the child in the Primary School is the chance to put his experience into words, to describe, to discuss, and to argue. If we offer him verbal teaching instead of his own doing, we deaden his mind; but on the other hand, if we deprive him of free speech with his fellows, we take away from him one of the most valuable means of intellectual and social growth. Active converse with his playmates and grown-up friends about his practical interests is the most natural spur towards clarity of thought and a sense of logic.

But how different would most of our classrooms be if we understood that! What we have done, and are still so often doing to-day, is to shut the school door on conversation—and yet, strangely enough, to look for ease and fluency in the written word. We insist on a dumb tongue, but hope for an eloquent pen! This is attempting to stride over one of the essential steps in the child's experience, and we deserve all the poverty of thought and expression which in fact we have got.

In the fourth place, it is the children's need for real activity that offers the chief justification for smaller classes, for modern individual methods, and for an organisation and grouping based upon the psychological study of individual differences (of which I wrote in earlier sections). So long as we rely upon the lecture method as our main device in teaching, we can group masses of children of disparate gifts together—and hardly find out how much we are wasting their time. But as soon as we realise that it is what *the children* do and say that educates them, and try to provide for activity, we are brought up against the differences between one child and another. There is little to be done with a large class of children, ranging in ability from the nearly defective to the very superior, but to keep them quiet and lecture to them. As we all know, the old conspiracy of silence and stillness arose from sheer necessity as much as from ignorance of child psychology. But when we make the groups smaller, and re-arrange them so that the members of any one group are roughly of the same level of general ability, it becomes more possible to let children have the free activity which is their breath of life.

Finally, it is when we get the full sense of this vital need for activity that the proper values of individual methods and of group methods in the school fall into just perspective. There is not really any question of choosing between these two types of method as a whole, but of seeing which is the more appropriate for particular purposes. In certain directions, individual methods will alone make it possible for all the children to be actively doing and thinking. This is very largely true of such things as the early stages of reading and writing, as arithmetic and geometry, and much historical and geographical study. It is true, too, of large parts of the more practical pursuits. In the making of real things, and in expressional drawing and modelling, far more interesting and effective work is done when each child follows out his own aims in his own time, than when all are forced into the same pattern.

There are other forms of activity, however, which are in their nature essentially communal, gaining most of their meaning and their beauty from *doing things together*. Such are, above all, dancing and singing and miming. But such in part, also, are gardening and the practical care of the schoolroom. And such may happily be, from time to time, particular projects in decorative art and constructional woodwork and needlework. But this does not mean all the children doing the same thing at the same time, as the old class methods demanded. It means, rather, each child making his own special contribution to the larger whole, itself a real and desired end. I suggested some possibilities of this type of co-operative activity (for instance, a decorative frieze for the classroom), when I was discussing social education.

If I have succeeded in stirring the interest of my readers in the practical working out of all these broad psychological truths, I shall feel that this little book has achieved its main purpose. I have not aimed at a systematic account of the psychology of childhood, of particular school subjects, or of detailed methods of teaching—but rather at describing some of the more significant characteristics of the mental development of children between seven and eleven years, and at showing how germane such facts are to the everyday work of the teacher.

Bibliography

P. B. Ballard GROUP TESTS OF INTELLIGENCE *University of London Press Ltd.* Cheap Edition, 1935.

P. B. Ballard MENTAL TESTS *University of London Press Ltd.* Cheap Edition, 1935.

P. B. Ballard THE NEW EXAMINER *University of London Press Ltd.* Cheap Edition, 1936.

A. Binet and Th. Simon MENTALLY DEFECTIVE CHILDREN *Edward Arnold.*

E. R. Boyce PLAY IN THE INFANTS' SCHOOL *Methuen*, 1938.

C. Burt MENTAL AND SCHOLASTIC TESTS *P. S. King & Son*, 1922.

C. Burt THE SUBNORMAL MIND *Oxford University Press*, 1935.

C. Burt THE BACKWARD CHILD *University of London Press Ltd*, 1938.

G. J. Cons and C. Fletcher ACTUALITY IN SCHOOL Methuen, 1938.

D. E. M. Gardner THE CHILDREN'S PLAY CENTRE *Methuen*, 1937.

D. E. M. Gardner TESTING RESULTS IN THE INFANT SCHOOL *Methuen*, 1942

H. R. Hamley (Edited by) THE TESTING OF INTELLIGENCE Evans Brothers, 1935.

H. R. Hamley (Edited by) THE EDUCATION OF BACKWARD CHILDREN *Evans Brothers*, 1936.

H. R. Hamley and others THE EDUCATIONAL GUIDANCE OF THE SCHOOL CHILD *Evans Brothers*, 1937.

D. Kennedy-Fraser THE EDUCATION OF THE BACKWARD CHILD *University of London Press Ltd*, 1931

S. Isaacs (Edited by) THE CAMBRIDGE EVACUATION
SURVEY *Methuen,* 1941.

S. Isaacs INTELLECTUAL GROWTH IN YOUNG CHILDREN
George Routledge & Sons, 1931; *Schocken Books,* 1966.

S. Isaacs SOCIAL DEVELOPMENT IN YOUNG CHILDREN
Routledge & Sons, 1933.

S. Isaacs THE PSYCHOLOGICAL ASPECTS OF CHILD
DEVELOPMENT *Evans Brothers,* 1935.

E. and M. Kenwrick THE CHILD FROM FIVE TO TEN
Kegan Paul, 1930.

Emmanuel Miller (Edited by) THE GROWING CHILD AND
ITS PROBLEMS *Kegan Paul,* 1937.

Sir T. P. Nunn EDUCATION: ITS DATA AND FIRST
PRINCIPLES *Edward Arnold.* Revised Edition, 1930.

J. Piaget THE MORAL JUDGMENT OF THE CHILD *Kegan
Paul,* 1932.

J. Piaget THE CHILD'S CONCEPTION OF THE WORLD
Kegan Paul, 1929.

J. Piaget JUDGMENT AND REASONING IN THE CHILD
Kegan Paul, 1928.

J. Piaget THE LANGUAGE AND THOUGHT OF THE CHILD
Kegan Paul, 1926.

V. Rasmussen THE PRIMARY SCHOOL CHILD *Gyldendal,*
1929.

J. Rickman (Edited by) CHILDREN IN WAR-TIME *New
Education Fellowship,* 1940

C. Spearman THE ABILITIES OF MAN *Macmillan,* 1927.

C. Spearman THE NATURE OF "INTELLIGENCE" AND THE
PRINCIPLES OF COGNITION *Macmillan,* 1923.

L. M. Terman THE MEASUREMENT OF INTELLIGENCE
Harrap & Co, 1919.

L. M. Terman and M. Lima CHILDREN'S READING
Appleton & Co, 1928.

Terman and Merrill MEASURING INTELLIGENCE *Harrap
& Co,* 1937.

E. B. Warr THE NEW ERA IN THE JUNIOR SCHOOL
Methuen, 1937.
Report of Consultative Committee of Board of Education THE
PRIMARY SCHOOL *His Majesty's Stationery Office,* 1931.

Index